THE GLENCOE LITERATURE LIBRARY

The Tempest

and Related Readings

New York, New York   Columbus, Ohio   Woodland Hills, California   Peoria, Illinois

Acknowledgments

Grateful acknowledgment is given authors, publishers, photographers, museums, and agents for permission to reprint the following copyrighted material. Every effort has been made to determine copyright owners. In case of any omissions, the Publisher will be pleased to make suitable acknowledgments in future editions.

"Two Control Freaks Take on Shakespeare," from A CONVERSATION WITH PATRICK STEWART AND GEORGE WOLFE reprinted by permission of the author Patrick R. Pacheco.

"*The Tempest* on Stage" by Robert Langbaum, from THE TEMPEST by William Shakespeare, edited by Robert Langbaum. Copyright © 1964, 1987 by Robert Langbaum. Used by permission of Dutton Signet, a division of Penguin Putman, Inc.

Excerpt from CALIBAN'S HOUR by Tad Williams, copyright © 1994 by Tad Williams. Reprinted by permission of HarperCollins Publishers, Inc. and Little, Brown and Company (UK).

Excerpt from "A Discovery of the Bermudas, Otherwise Called the Isle of Devils," in A VOYAGE TO VIRGINIA IN 1609 by Louis B. Wright, ed. Copyright © 1964 by The Rector and Visitors of The University of Virginia. Reprinted by permission.

Text excerpt "Those Huddled Masses" by Tim Clark, pp. 11–16, as seen in *The Perilous Sea* edited by Clarissa M. Silitch, Yankee Books, 1985.

Cover Art: *Miranda—The Tempest*, 1916. John William Waterhouse (1849–1917). Oil on canvas, 100.5 x 137 cm. Private collection. Sotheby's Picture Library.

Glencoe/McGraw-Hill

A Division of The ***McGraw-Hill*** *Companies*

Send all inquiries to:
Glencoe/McGraw-Hill
8787 Orion Place
Columbus, OH 43240

ISBN 0-02-817988-9
Printed in the United States of America
1 2 3 4 5 6 7 8 9 026 04 03 02 01 00

Contents

Continued

Contents Continued

The Tempest

William Shakespeare

Cast of Characters

PROSPERO: the rightful Duke of Milan

MIRANDA: his daughter

ANTONIO: his brother, the usurping Duke of Milan

ALONSO: King of Naples

SEBASTIAN: his brother

FERDINAND: Alonso's son

GONZALO: an honest old counsellor of Naples

ADRIAN: } lords
FRANCISCO: }

ARIEL: an airy spirit attendant upon Prospero

CALIBAN: a savage and deformed native of the island, Prospero's slave

TRINCULO: Alonso's jester

STEFANO: Alonso's drunken butler

MASTER: captain of Antonio's ship

BOATSWAIN, MARINERS, SPIRITS

THE MASQUE

Spirits appearing as:

IRIS

CERES

JUNO

NYMPHS, REAPERS

Act 1

Scene 1

[*A tempestuous noise of thunder and lightning heard. Enter a* SHIPMASTER *and a* BOATSWAIN *at separate doors*.]

MASTER. Boatswain!°

BOATSWAIN. Here, Master. What cheer?°

MASTER. Good,° speak to th' mariners. Fall to't yarely,° or we run ourselves aground. Bestir,° bestir!

[*Exit. Enter* MARINERS.]

5 **BOATSWAIN.** Heigh, my hearts!° Cheerly,° cheerly, my hearts! Yare, yare! Take in the topsail! Tend° to th' Master's whistle!—
Blow till thou burst thy wind, if room enough.

[*Enter* ALONSO, SEBASTIAN, ANTONIO, FERDINAND, GONZALO *and others*.]

ALONSO. Good Boatswain, have care. Where's the Master?
[*To the* MARINERS.] Play the men!°

10 **BOATSWAIN.** I pray now, keep below.

ANTONIO. Where is the Master, Boatswain?

BOATSWAIN. Do you not hear him? You mar our labour. Keep your cabins; you do assist the storm.

---

1 **Boatswain** a ship's officer

2 **What cheer** How are you?

3 **Good** good man;
Fall to't yarely proceed quickly

4 **Bestir** get moving

5 **hearts** hearties;
Cheerly heartily

6 **Tend** pay attention

9 **Play the men** behave like men

GONZALO. Nay, good,° be patient.

15 **BOATSWAIN.** When the sea is. Hence! What cares these roarers for the name of the king?° To cabin! Silence; trouble us not.

GONZALO. Good, yet remember whom thou hast aboard.

BOATSWAIN. None that I more love than myself. You are a councillor;° if you can command these elements to silence and work
20 peace of the present, we will not hand° a rope more. Use your authority. If you cannot, give thanks you have lived so long and make yourself ready in your cabin for the mischance of the hour, if it so hap.° [*To the* MARINERS.] Cheerly, good hearts! [*To* GONZALO.] Out of our way, I say!

[*The* BOATSWAIN *exits.*]

25 **GONZALO.** I have great comfort from this fellow. Methinks he hath no drowning mark upon him; his complexion is perfect gallows. Stand fast, good Fate, to his hanging. Make the rope of his destiny our cable, for our own doth little advantage. If he be not born to be hanged, our case is miserable.

[*Exit Courtiers. Enter* BOATSWAIN.]

30 **BOATSWAIN.** Down with the topmast! Yare! Lower, lower! Bring her to try wi'th' main-course!

[*A cry within.*]

A plague upon this howling! They are louder than the weather, or our office.

[*Enter* SEBASTIAN, ANTONIO, *and* GONZALO.]

Yet again? What do you here? Shall we give o'er° and drown?
35 Have you a mind to sink?

SEBASTIAN. A pox o'your throat, you bawling, blasphemous, incharitable dog!

BOATSWAIN. Work you, then.

ANTONIO. Hang, cur, hang, you whoreson insolent noisemaker.
40 We are less afraid to be drowned than thou art.

---

14 **good** good fellow
15–16 **What cares . . . king** Wind and waves don't care about rank
18 **councillor** member of the King's council
20 **hand** handle
23 **hap** happen
34 **give o'er** give up

[*Exeunt* MARINERS.]

GONZALO. I'll warrant him for° drowning, though the ship were no stronger than a nutshell and as leaky as an unstanched wench.

BOATSWAIN. Lay her a-hold, a-hold! Set her two courses! Off to
45 sea again! Lay her off!

[*Enter* MARINERS, *wet*.]

MARINERS. All lost! To prayers, to prayers! All lost!

[*Exeunt* MARINERS.]

BOATSWAIN. What, must our mouths be cold?

GONZALO. The King and Prince at prayers! Let's assist them,
For our case is as theirs.

SEBASTIAN. I'm out of patience.

50 **ANTONIO.** We are merely° cheated of our lives by drunkards,
This wide-chopped rascal—would thou mightst lie drowning
The washing of ten tides.

GONZALO. He'll be hanged yet,
Though every drop of water swear against it
And gape at wid'st to glut him.

[*A confused noise within*.]

MARINERS. [*Within*.] Mercy on us!
55 We split, we split! Farewell, my wife and children!
Farewell, brother! We split, we split, we split!

[*Exit* BOATSWAIN.]

ANTONIO. Let's all sink wi'th' King.

SEBASTIAN. Let's take leave of him.

[*Exit* ANTONIO *and* SEBASTIAN.]

GONZALO. Now would I give a thousand furlongs of sea for an acre of barren ground: long heath, broom, furze,° anything.
60 The wills above be done, but I would fain° die a dry death.

[*Exit*.]

---

41 **warrant him for** guarantee him against
50 **merely** utterly
59 **long heath, broom, furze** shrubs that grow in poor soil
60 **fain** gladly

Scene 2

[*Enter* PROSPERO *(in his magic cloak, with a staff) and* MIRANDA.]

MIRANDA. If by your art,° my dearest father, you have
Put the wild waters in this roar, allay° them.
The sky, it seems, would pour down stinking pitch,°
But that the sea, mounting to th' welkin's° cheek,
5 Dashes the fire out. O, I have sufferèd
With those that I saw suffer! A brave vessel,
Who had, no doubt, some noble creature in her,
Dashed all to pieces! O, the cry did knock
Against my very heart! Poor souls, they perished.
10 Had I been any god of power, I would
Have sunk the sea within the earth, or ere°
It should the good ship so have swallowed and
The fraughting souls° within her.

PROSPERO. Be collected.
No more amazement.° Tell your piteous° heart
15 There's no harm done.

MIRANDA. O woe the day!

PROSPERO. No harm.
I have done nothing but in care of thee,
Of thee, my dear one, thee, my daughter, who
Art ignorant of what thou art, naught knowing
Of whence I am, nor that I am more better°
20 Than Prospero, master of a full poor cell°
And thy no greater father.

MIRANDA. More to know
Did never meddle with° my thoughts.

---

1 **art** magic
2 **allay** calm
3 **pitch** tar
4 **welkin's** sky's
11 **or ere** before
13 **fraughting souls** passengers
14 **amazement** bewilderment;
piteous pitying
19 **more better** of higher rank
20 **full poor cell** very humble cottage
22 **meddle with** enter

PROSPERO. 'Tis time
I should inform thee farther. Lend thy hand,
And pluck my magic garment from me.

[*MIRANDA removes PROSPERO's cloak, and he lays it on the ground.*]

So.
25 Lie there, my art.—Wipe thou thine eyes; have comfort.
The direful spectacle of the wreck, which touched
The very virtue of compassion in thee,
I have with such provision° in mine art
So safely ordered that there is no soul—
30 No, not so much perdition° as an hair
Betid° to any creature in the vessel,
Which thou heard'st cry, which thou saw'st sink. Sit down,
For thou must now know farther.

[*MIRANDA sits.*]

MIRANDA. You have often
Begun to tell me what I am, but stopped
35 And left me to a bootless inquisition°
Concluding 'Stay; not yet'.

PROSPERO. The hour's now come
The very minute bids thee ope° thine ear,
Obey, and be attentive. Canst thou remember
A time before we came unto this cell?
40 I do not think thou canst, for then thou wast not
Out° three years old.

MIRANDA. Certainly, sir, I can.

PROSPERO. By what? By any other house or person?
Of anything the image tell me that
Hath kept with thy remembrance.

MIRANDA. 'Tis far off,
45 And rather like a dream than an assurance°

---

28 **provision** foresight
30 **perdition** loss
31 **Betid** happened
35 **bootless inquisition** useless inquiry
37 **ope** open
41 **Out** fully
45 **an assurance** a certainty

That my remembrance warrants.° Had I not
Four or five women once that tended me?

PROSPERO. Thou hadst, and more, Miranda. But how is it
That this lives in thy mind? What seest thou else
50 In the dark backward° and abyss of time?
If thou rememb'rest aught ere° thou cam'st here,
How thou cam'st here thou mayst.

MIRANDA. But that I do not.

PROSPERO. Twelve year since, Miranda, twelve year since,
Thy father was the Duke of Milan, and
55 A prince of power—

MIRANDA. Sir, are not you my father?

PROSPERO. Thy mother was a piece of virtue, and
She said thou wast my daughter; and thy father
Was Duke of Milan, and his only heir
And princess no worse issued.°

MIRANDA. O the heavens!
60 What foul play had we that we came from thence?
Or blessèd was't we did?

PROSPERO. Both, both, my girl.
By foul play, as thou sayst, were we heaved thence,
But blessedly holp° hither.

MIRANDA. O, my heart bleeds
To think o'th' teen° that I have turned you to,
65 Which is from° my remembrance. Please you, farther.

PROSPERO. My brother and thy uncle called Antonio—
I pray thee mark me, that a brother should
Be so perfidious°—he whom next° thyself
Of all the world I loved, and to him put

---

46 **warrants** guarantees to be true

50 **backward** past

51 **aught ere** anything before

59 **no worse issued** no less nobly born

63 **holp** helped

64 **o'th' teen** of the trouble

65 **from** absent from

68 **perfidious** treacherous;
next after

70 The manage of my state—as at that time
Through all the signories° it was the first,
And Prospero the prime duke—being so reputed
In dignity, and for the liberal arts
Without a parallel—those being all my study,
75 The government I cast upon my brother,
And to my state grew stranger, being transported°
And rapt° in secret studies. Thy false uncle—
Dost thou attend me?

MIRANDA. Sir, most heedfully.

PROSPERO. Being once perfected how to grant suits,°
80 How to deny them, who t'advance and who
To trash for over-topping,° new created
The creatures° that were mine, I say—or changed 'em
Or else new formed 'em,° having both the key
Of officer and office, set all hearts i'th' state
85 To what tune pleased his ear, that now he was
The ivy which had hid my princely trunk
And sucked my verdure° out on't. Thou attend'st not!

MIRANDA. O good sir, I do.

PROSPERO. I pray thee mark me.
I, thus neglecting wordly ends, all dedicated
90 To closeness° and the bettering of my mind
With that which but° by being so retired
O'er-priced all popular rate,° in my false brother
Awaked an evil nature; and my trust,
Like a good parent, did beget of him
95 A falsehood, in its contrary as great
As my trust was, which had indeed no limit,

---

71 **signories** lordships
76 **transported** carried away
77 **rapt** enraptured
79 **Being once perfected . . . suits** having mastered the granting of petitions
81 **trash for over-topping** restrain for overambition
82 **creatures** dependent officials
82–83 **or changed . . . formed 'em** changed their allegiance or created new officials
87 **verdure** sap; vitality
90 **closeness** privacy
91 **but** merely
92 **O'er-priced . . . rate** exceeded the public's understanding

A confidence sans bound.° He being thus lorded
Not only with what my revenue yielded
But what my power might else exact, like one
100 Who having into truth, by telling oft,
Made such a sinner of his memory
To credit his own lie, he did believe
He was indeed the Duke. Out o'th'° substitution,
And executing th'outward face° of royalty
105 With all prerogative, hence his ambition growing—
Dost thou hear?

MIRANDA. Your tale, sir, would cure deafness.

PROSPERO. To have no screen between this part he played
And him he played it for, he needs will be
Absolute Milan. Me, poor man—my library
110 Was dukedom large enough—of temporal royalties°
He thinks me now incapable; confederates,°
So dry° he was for sway,° wi'th' King of Naples
To give him annual tribute, do him homage,
Subject his coronet° to his crown, and bend
115 The dukedom, yet unbowed—alas, poor Milan—
To most ignoble stooping.

MIRANDA. O the heavens!

PROSPERO. Mark his condition and th'event, then tell me
If this might be a brother.

MIRANDA. I should sin
To think but nobly of my grandmother.
120 Good wombs have borne bad sons.

PROSPERO. Now the condition.
This King of Naples, being an enemy
To me inveterate, hearkens my brother's suit;
Which was that he, in lieu o'th' premises

---

97 **sans bound** without limit

103 **Out o'th'** as a consequence of

104 **executing th' outward face** fulfilling the outward appearance

110 **temporal royalties** exercise of worldly power

111 **confederates** forms an alliance

112 **dry** thirsty;
sway power

114 **coronet** crown worn by a nobleman rather than a king

Of homage and I know not how much tribute,
125 Should presently extirpate me and mine
Out of the dukedom, and confer fair Milan,
With all the honours, on my brother. Whereon,
A treacherous army levied, one midnight
Fated to th' purpose did Antonio open
130 The gates of Milan; and, i'th' dead of darkness,
The ministers for th' purpose hurried thence
Me and thy crying self.

MIRANDA. Alack, for pity!
I, not rememb'ring how I cried out then,
Will cry it o'er again; it is a hint°
135 That wrings mine eyes to't.

PROSPERO. [*Sitting.*] Hear a little further,
And then I'll bring thee to the present business
Which now's upon's, without the which this story
Were most impertinent.°

MIRANDA. Wherefore did they not
That hour destroy us?

PROSPERO. Well demanded, wench°
140 My tale provokes that question. Dear, they durst not,
So dear the love my people bore me; nor set
A mark so bloody on the business, but
With colours fairer painted their foul ends.
In few,° they hurried us aboard a barque,°
145 Bore us some leagues to sea, where they prepared
A rotten carcass of a butt,° not rigged,
Nor tackle, sail, nor mast—the very rats
Instictively have quit it. There they hoist us,
To cry to th' sea that roared to us, to sigh
150 To th'winds, whose pity, sighing back again,
Did us but loving wrong.

MIRANDA. Alack, what trouble
Was I then to you!

---

134 **hint** occasion

138 **impertinent** irrelevant

139 **wench** used here as a term of endearment for a daughter

144 **few** brief;
barque ship

146 **butt** barrel or tub

PROSPERO. O, a cherubin
Thou wast that did preserve me. Thou didst smile,
Infusèd with a fortitude from heaven,
155 When I have decked° the sea with drops full salt,
Under my burden groaned, which raised in me
An undergoing stomach, to bear up
Against what should ensue.

MIRANDA. How came we ashore?

160 **PROSPERO.** By providence divine.
Some food we had, and some fresh water that
A noble Neapolitan, Gonzalo,
Out of his charity—who being then appointed
Master of this design—did give us; with
165 Rich garments, linens, stuffs and necessaries
Which since have steaded much.° So, of his gentleness,°
Knowing I loved my books, he furnished me
From mine own library with volumes that
I prize above my dukedom.

MIRANDA. Would I might
170 But ever see that man!

PROSPERO. Now I arise.

[*He stands and puts on his cloak.*]

Sit still, and hear the last of our sea-sorrow.
Here in this island we arrived, and here
Have I thy schoolmaster made thee more profit°
Than other princes can, that have more time
175 For vainer hours and tutors not so careful.

MIRANDA. Heavens thank you for't. And now I pray you, sir—
For still 'tis beating in my mind—your reason
For raising this sea-storm.

PROSPERO. Know thus far forth.
By accident most strange, bountiful Fortune,
180 Now my dear lady, hath mine enemies
Brought to this shore; and by my prescience
I find my zenith doth depend upon

---

155 **decked** adorned

166 **have steaded much** have been very useful;
gentleness nobility

173 **made thee more profit** made you profit more

A most auspicious star, whose influence
If now I court not, but omit, my fortunes
185 Will ever after droop. Here cease more questions.
Thou art inclined to sleep; 'tis a good dullness,°
And give it way. I know thou canst not choose.

[MIRANDA *sleeps*.]

Come away, servant, come! I am ready now.
Approach, my Ariel, come!

[*Enter* ARIEL.]

190 **ARIEL.** All hail, great master, grave sir, hail. I come
To answer thy best pleasure. Be't to fly,
To swim, to dive into the fire, to ride
On the curled clouds, to thy strong bidding task
Ariel and all his quality.°

PROSPERO. Hast thou, spirit,
195 Performed to point° the tempest that I bade thee?

ARIEL. To every article.
I boarded the King's ship. Now on the beak,°
Now in the waste,° the deck, in every cabin,
I flamed amazement.° Sometime I'd divide,
200 And burn in many places, on the top-mast,
The yards, and bowsprit, would I flame distinctly;
Then meet and join. Jove's lightning, the precursors
O'th' dreadful thunderclaps, more momentary
And sight-outrunning° were not. The fire and cracks
205 Of sulphurous roaring the most mighty Neptune°
Seem to besiege, and make his bold waves tremble,
Yea, his dread trident shake.

---

186 **dullness** drowsiness
194 **quality** abilities or fellow spirits
195 **to point** in exact detail
197 **beak** prow
198 **waste** central part of the ship
199 **flamed amazement** caused terror by appearing as a flame
204 **sight-outrunning** quicker than the eye
205 **Neptune** mythological god of the sea

PROSPERO. My brave spirit!
Who was so firm, so constant, that this coil°
Would not infect his reason?

ARIEL. Not a soul
210 But felt a fever of the mad, and played
Some tricks of desperation. All but mariners
Plunged in the foaming brine and quit the vessel,
Then all afire with me. The King's son Ferdinand,
With hair upstarting°—then like reeds, not hair—
215 Was the first man that leaped; cried 'Hell is empty,
And all the devils are here'.

PROSPERO. Why, that's my spirit!
But was not this nigh shore?

ARIEL. Close by, my master.

PROSPERO. But are they, Ariel, safe?

ARIEL. Not a hair perished.
On their sustaining garments° not a blemish,
220 But fresher than before. And, as thou bad'st° me,
In troops I have dispersed them 'bout the isle.
The King's son have I landed by himself.
Whom I left cooling of the air with sighs
In an odd angle° of the isle, and sitting,
His arms in this sad knot.°

225 PROSPERO. Of the King's ship,
The mariners, say how thou hast disposed,
And all the rest o'th' fleet.

ARIEL. Safely in harbour
Is the King's ship, in the deep nook where once
Thou called'st me up at midnight to fetch dew
230 From the still-vexed° Bermudas, there she's hid;
The mariners all under hatches stowed,
Who, with a charm joined to their suffered labour,

---

208 **coil** turmoil
214 **upstaring** standing up
219 **sustaining garments** garments that helped them float to shore
220 **bad'st** badest; commanded
224 **odd angle** out-of-the-way corner
225 **in this sad knot** folded sadly (Ariel demonstrates)
230 **still vexed** always stormy

I have left asleep. And for the rest o'th' fleet,
Which I dispersed, they all have met again,
235 And are upon the Mediterranean float°
Bound sadly home for Naples,
Supposing that they saw the King's ship wrecked,
And his great person perish.

PROSPERO. Ariel, thy charge
Exactly is performed; but there's more work.
240 What is the time o'th' day?

ARIEL. Past the mid season.°

PROSPERO. At least two glasses.° The time 'twixt six and now
Must by us both be spent most preciously.

ARIEL. Is there more toil? Since thou dost give me pains,°
Let me remember° thee what thou hast promised
245 Which is not yet performed me.

PROSPERO. How now? Moody?
What is't thou canst demand?

ARIEL. My liberty.

PROSPERO. Before the time be out? No more!

ARIEL. I prithee,°
Remember I have done thee worthy service,
Told thee no lies, made thee no mistakings, served
250 Without or grudge or grumblings. Thou did promise
To bate me° a full year.

PROSPERO. Dost thou forget
From what a torment I did free thee?

ARIEL. No.

PROSPERO. Thou dost, and think'st it much to tread the ooze
Of the salt deep,
255 To run upon the sharp wind of the north,

---

235 **float** sea
240 **mid season** noon
241 **two glasses** two o'clock (two hourglasses past noon)
243 **pains** tasks
244 **remember** remind
247 **I prithee** I beg of you
251 **bate me** deduct from the period of my service

To do me business in the veins o'th' earth°
When it is baked° with frost.

ARIEL. I do not, sir.

PROSPERO. Thou liest, malignant thing. Hast thou forgot
The foul witch Sycorax, who with age and envy
260 Was grown into a hoop?° Hast thou forgot her?

ARIEL. No, sir.

PROSPERO. Thou hast. Where was she born? Speak, tell me!

ARIEL. Sir, in Algiers.

PROSPERO. O, was she so! I must
Once in a month recount what thou hast been,
265 Which thou forget'st. This damned witch Sycorax,
For mischiefs manifold and sorceries terrible
To enter human hearing, from Algiers
Thou know'st was banished. For one thing she did
They would not take her life. Is this not true?

270 **ARIEL.** Ay, sir.

PROSPERO. This blue-eyed° hag was hither brought with child,
And here was left by th' sailors. Thou, my slave,
As thou report'st thyself, was then her servant;
And for thou wast a spirit too delicate
275 To act her earthy° and abhorred commands,
Refusing her grand hests,° she did confine thee
By help of her more potent ministers,
And in her most unmitigable rage,
Into a cloven pine; within which rift
280 Imprisoned thou didst painfully remain
A dozen years, within which space she died
And left thee there, where thou didst vent thy groans
As fast as mill-wheels strike.° Then was this island—
Save for the son that she did litter° here,

---

256 **veins o'th' earth** mineral veins or underground streams
257 **baked** hardened
260 **grown into a hoop** bent over
271 **blue-eyed** Blue eyelids, thought to be a sign of pregnancy
275 **earthy** in contrast with Ariel's airy nature
276 **hests** commands
283 **as mill-wheels strike** as the blades of mill wheels hit the water
284 **litter** give birth to

285 A freckled whelp, hag-born—not honoured with
A human shape.

ARIEL. Yes, Caliban, her son.

PROSPERO. Dull thing, I say so. He, that Caliban
Whom now I keep in service. Thou best know'st
What torment I did find thee in. Thy groans
290 Did make wolves howl, and penetrate the breasts°
Of ever-angry bears; it was a torment
To lay upon the damned, which Sycorax
Could not again undo. It was mine art,
When I arrived and heard thee, that made gape
295 The pine and let thee out.

ARIEL. I thank thee, master.

PROSPERO. If thou more murmur'st, I will rend an oak,
And peg thee in his knotty entrails till
Thou has howled away twelve winters.

ARIEL. Pardon, master.
I will be correspondent° to command,
300 And do my spriting gently.°

PROSPERO. Do so, and after two days
I will discharge thee.

ARIEL. That's my noble master!
What shall I do? Say what, what shall I do?

PROSPERO. Go make thyself like to a nymph o'th' sea. Be subject
305 To no sight but thine and mine, invisible
To every eyeball else. Go take this shape,
And hither come in't. Go; hence with diligence!

[*Exit* ARIEL.]

Awake, dear heart, awake! Thou has slept well;
Awake.

MIRANDA. [*Awaking.*] The strangeness of your story put
310 Heaviness° in me.

---

290 **penetrate the breasts** arouse sympathy in

299 **correspondent** obedient

300 **do my spriting gently** do my spiriting graciously

309 **Heaviness** drowsiness

PROSPERO. Shake it off. Come on;
We'll visit Caliban my slave, who never
Yields us kind answer.

MIRANDA. 'Tis a villain, sir,
I do not love to look on.

PROSPERO. But as 'tis,
We cannot miss° him. He does make our fire,
315 Fetch in our wood, and serves in offices
That profit us—What ho! Slave, Caliban!
Thou earth, thou, speak!

CALIBAN. [*Within.*] There's wood enough within.

PROSPERO. Come forth, I say! There's other business for thee.
Come, thou tortoise! When?

[*Enter* ARIEL, *like a water-nymph.*]

320 Fine apparition! My quaint Ariel,
Hark in thine ear.

[*He whispers.*]

ARIEL. My lord, it shall be done.

[*Exit.*]

PROSPERO. Thou poisonous slave, got by the devil himself
Upon thy wicked dam,° come forth!

[*Enter* CALIBAN.]

CALIBAN. As wicked dew° as e'er my mother brushed
325 With raven's feather from unwholesome fen°
Drop on you both! A southwest° blow on ye,
And blister you all o'er!

PROSPERO. For this be sure tonight thou shalt have cramps,
Side-stitches that shall pen thy breath up. Urchins°
330 Shall forth at vast° of night, that they may work
All exercise on thee. Thou shalt be pinched

---

314 **miss** do without
323 **dam** mother
324 **dew** a common ingredient in magical potions
325 **fen** bog
326 **southwest** wind that carries disease
329 **urchins** goblins in the shape of hedgehogs
330 **at vast** during the long stretch

As thick as honeycomb, each pinch more stinging
Than bees that made 'em.

CALIBAN. I must eat my dinner.
This island's mine, by Sycorax my mother,
335 Which thou tak'st from me. When thou cam'st first,
Thou strok'st me and made much of me, wouldst give me
Water with berries in't, and teach me how
To name the bigger light,° and how the less,°
That burn by day and night; and then I loved thee,
340 And showed thee all the qualities o'th' isle,
The fresh springs, brine-pits, barren place and fertile—
Cursed be that I did so! All the charms°
Of Sycorax, toads, beetles, bats, light on you;
For I am all the subjects that you have,
345 Which first was mine own king, and here you sty me°
In this hard rock, whiles you do keep from me
The rest o'th' island.

PROSPERO. Thou most lying slave
Whom stripes° may move, not kindness! I have used° thee,
Filth as thou art, with human care, and lodged thee
350 In mine own cell, till thou didst seek to violate
The honour of my child.

CALIBAN. O ho, O ho! Would't had been done!
Thou didst prevent me, I had peopled else
This isle with Calibans.

MIRANDA. Abhorrèd slave,
355 Which any print of goodness will not take,
Being capable of all ill! I pitied thee,
Took pains to make thee speak, taught thee each hour
One thing or other. When thou didst not, savage,
Know thine own meaning, but wouldst gabble like
360 A thing most brutish, I endowed thy purposes
With words that made them known. But thy vile race,°

---

338 **bigger light** the sun;
the less the moon

342 **charms** spells

345 **sty me** pen me up like a pig

348 **stripes** lashes;
used treated

361 **race** nature

Though thou didst learn, had that in't which good natures
Could not abide to be with; therefore wast thou
Deservedly confined into this rock,
365 Who hadst deserved more than a prison.

CALIBAN. You taught me language, and my profit on't
Is I know how to curse. The red plague° rid° you
For learning me your language!

PROSPERO. Hag-seed,° hence!
Fetch us in fuel. And be quick, thou'rt best,
370 To answer other business.°—Shrug'st thou, malice?
If thou neglect'st or dost unwillingly
What I command, I'll rack thee with old cramps,
Fill all thy bones with aches, make thee roar,
That beasts shall tremble at thy din.

CALIBAN. No, pray thee.
375 [*Aside.*] I must obey. His art is of such power
It would control my dam's god Setebos,°
And make a vassal° of him.

PROSPERO. So, slave, hence!

[*Exit* CALIBAN. *Enter* FERDINAND *and* ARIEL, *invisible, playing and singing.* PROSPERO *and* MIRANDA *stand aside.*]

[*Song.*]

ARIEL. Come unto these yellow sands,
And then take hands;
380 Curtsied when you have and kissed—
The wild waves whist°—
Foot it featly° here and there,
And, sweet sprites, bear
The burden.° Hark, hark.

385 **SPIRITS.** [*Dispersedly within.*] Bow-wow!

---

367 **red plague** plague that causes red sores;
rid kill

368 **Hag-seed** witch's offspring

370 **answer other business** perform other tasks

376 **Setebos** a god worshipped in Patagonia, South America

377 **vassal** servant

381 **whist** fall silent

382 **Foot it featly** dance nimbly

383–384 **bear . . . burden** sing the refrain

ARIEL. The watch-dogs bark.

SPIRITS. [*Within.*] Bow-wow!

ARIEL. Hark, hark, I hear
The strain° of strutting Chanticleer°
390 Cry 'cock-a-diddle-dow'.

FERDINAND. Where should this music be? I'th' air or th' earth?
It sounds no more; and sure it waits upon
Some god o'th' island. Sitting on a bank,
Weeping again the King my father's wreck,
395 This music crept by me upon the waters,
Allaying both their fury and my passion°
With its sweet air.° Thence I have followed it—
Or it hath drawn me rather. But 'tis gone.
No, it begins again.

[*Song.*]

400 **ARIEL.** Full fathom five° thy father lies.
Of his bones are coral made;
These are pearls that were his eyes;
Nothing of him that doth fade
But doth suffer a sea-change
405 Into something rich and strange,
Sea-nymphs hourly ring his knell:°

SPIRITS. [*Within.*] Ding dong.

ARIEL. Hark, now I hear them.

SPIRITS. [*Within.*] Ding-dong bell. [*etc.*]

FERDINAND. The ditty° does remember° my drowned father.
410 This is no mortal° business, nor no sound

---

389 **strain** song;
Chanticleer the name of a rooster

396 **passion** grief, suffering

397 **air** melody

400 **Full fathom five** five fathoms, or thirty feet deep

406 **knell** the sound of a funeral bell

409 **ditty** song;
remember commemorate

410 **mortal** human

That the earth owes.°

[*Music.*]

I hear it now above me.

PROSPERO. [*To* MIRANDA.] The fringèd curtains of thine eye advance,°
And say what thou seest yon.

MIRANDA. What is't? A spirit?
Lord, how it looks about! Believe me, sir
415 It carries a brave form. But 'tis a spirit.

PROSPERO. No, wench, it eats and sleeps, and hath such sense
As we have, such. This gallant° which thou seest
Was in the wreck, and but he's something stained
With grief, that's beauty's canker,° thou mightst call him
420 A goodly person. He hath lost his fellows,
And strays about to find 'em.

MIRANDA. I might call him
A thing divine, for nothing natural
I ever saw so noble.

PROSPERO. [*Aside.*] It goes on,° I see,
As my soul prompts it. [*To* ARIEL.] Spirit, fine spirit, I'll free thee
Within two days for this.

425 **FERDINAND.** [*Aside.*] Most sure the goddess
On whom these airs attend. [*To* MIRANDA.] Vouchsafe° my prayer
May know° if you remain° upon this island,
And that you will some good instruction give
How I may bear me° here. My prime request,
430 Which I do last pronounce, is—O you wonder—
If you be maid° or no?

---

411 **owes** owns
412 **advance** raise
417 **gallant** fashionable gentleman
419 **canker** a corrupting sore
423 **It goes on** my plan proceeds
426 **Vouchsafe** grant
427 **May know** that I may know;
remain dwell
429 **bear me** conduct myself
431 **maid** a girl (as opposed to a supernatural being)

MIRANDA. No wonder, sir,
But certainly a maid.

FERDINAND. My language! Heavens!
I am the best° of them that speak this speech,
Were I but where 'tis spoken.

PROSPERO. How, the best?
435 What wert thou if the King of Naples heard thee?

FERDINAND. A single thing, as I am now that wonders
To hear thee speak of Naples. He does hear me,
And that he does I weep. Myself am Naples,°
Who with mine eyes, never since at ebb,° beheld
440 The king my father wrecked.

MIRANDA. Alack, for mercy!

FERDINAND. Yes, faith, and all his lords, the Duke of Milan
And his brave son being twain.

PROSPERO. [*Aside.*] The Duke of Milan
And his more braver daughter could control° thee,
If now 'twere fit to do't. At the first sight
445 They have changed eyes°—Delicate° Ariel,
I'll set thee free for this. [*To* FERDINAND.] A word, good sir.
I fear you have done yourself some wrong.° A word.

MIRANDA. [*Aside.*] Why speaks my father so ungently? This
Is the third man that e'er I saw, the first
450 That e'er I sighed for. Pity move my father
To be inclined my way.

FERDINAND. O, if a virgin,
And your affection not gone forth,° I'll make you
The Queen of Naples.

PROSPERO. Soft,° sir! One word more.

---

433 **the best** highest in rank

438 **Naples** King of Naples

439 **never since at ebb** continually weeping

443 **control** contradict

445 **changed eyes** exchanged loving looks;
delicate graceful, artful

447 **done yourself some wrong** spoken in error

452 **your affection not gone forth** not already in love with someone else

453 **Soft** Wait a minute

[*Aside*.] They are both in either's powers. But this swift business
455 I must uneasy° make, lest too light winning
Make the prize light.° [*To* FERDINAND.] One word more. I charge thee
That thou attend me. Thou dost here usurp
The name thou ow'st° not; and hast put thyself
Upon this island as a spy, to win it
From me the lord on't.

460 **FERDINAND.** No, as I am a man.

MIRANDA. There's nothing ill can dwell in such a temple.°
If the ill spirit have so fair a house,
Good things will strive to dwell with't.

PROSPERO. [*To* FERDINAND.] Follow me.
[*To* MIRANDA.] Speak not you for him; he's a traitor. [*To* FERDINAND.] Come!
465 I'll manacle thy neck and feet together.
Sea-water shalt thou drink; thy food shall be
The fresh-brook mussels,° withered roots and husks
Wherein the acorn cradled. Follow!

FERDINAND. No.
I will resist such entertainment° till
470 Mine enemy has more power.

[*He draws, and is charmed from moving*.]

MIRANDA. O dear father,
Make not too rash a trial° of him, for
He's gentle,° and nor fearful.

PROSPERO. What, I say,
My foot my tutor?° Put thy sword up, traitor,
Who mak'st a show but dar'st not strike, thy conscience

---

455 **uneasy** difficult
456 **light** cheap
458 **ow'st** own
461 **temple** Antonio's handsome exterior
467 **fresh-brook mussels** inedible freshwater mussels
469 **entertainment** treatment
471 **rash a trial** strong a test
472 **gentle** noble
473 **My foot my tutor?** Should I let my inferior guide me?

475 Is so possessed with guilt. Come from thy ward,°
For I can here disarm thee with this stick°
And make thy weapon drop.

MIRANDA. Beseech you, father!

PROSPERO. Hence! Hang not on my garments.

MIRANDA. Sir, have pity.
I'll be his surety.

PROSPERO. Silence! One word more
480 Shall make me chide thee, if not hate thee. What,
An advocate for an imposter? Hush!
Thou think'st there is no more such shapes as he,
Having seen but him and Caliban. Foolish wench!
To° th' most of men this is a Caliban,
485 And they to him are angels.

MIRANDA. My affections
Are then most humble. I have no ambition
To see a goodlier man.

PROSPERO. [*To* FERDINAND.] Come on; obey.
Thy nerves° are in their again,
And have no vigour in them.

FERDINAND. So they are.
490 My spirits, as in a dream, are all bound up.
My father's loss, the weakness which I feel,
The wreck of all my friends, nor this man's threats
To whom I am subdued, are but light° to me,
Might I but through my prison once a day
495 Behold this maid. All corners else° o'th' earth
Let liberty make use of; space enough
Have I in such a prison.

PROSPERO. [*Aside.*] It works. [*To* ARIEL.] Come on.—
Thou hast done well, fine Ariel. [*To* FERDINAND.] Follow me.
[*To* ARIEL.] Hark what thou else shalt do me.

---

475 **ward** fencer's defensive posture
476 **stick** magician's staff
484 **To** compared to
488 **nerves** sinews (Ferdinand is as helpless as a baby.)
493 **but light** only of little importance
495 **All corners else** all other places

MIRANDA [*To* FERDINAND.] Be of comfort.

500 My father's of a better nature, sir.
Than he appears by speech. This is unwonted°
Which now came from him.

PROSPERO. [*To* ARIEL.] Thou shalt be as free
As mountain winds, but then° exactly do
All points of my command.

505 **ARIEL.** To th' syllable.

PROSPERO. [*To* FERDINAND.] Come, follow. [*To* MIRANDA.] Speak not for him.

[*Exeunt.*]

---

501 **unwonted** unusual

503 **then** if that is to happen

Act 2

Scene 1

[*Enter* ALONSO, SEBASTIAN, ANTONIO, GONZALO, ADRIAN, *and* FRANCISCO.]

GONZALO. [*To* ALONSO.] Beseech you, sir, be merry. You have cause,
So have we all, of joy; for our escape
Is much beyond our loss. Our hint° of woe
Is common; every day some sailor's wife,
5 The masters of some merchant, and the merchant,
Have just our theme of woe. But for the miracle,
I mean our preservation, few in millions
Can speak like us. Then wisely, good sir, weigh
Our sorrow with our comfort.

ALONSO. Prithee, peace.

10 **SEBASTIAN.** [*To* ANTONIO.] He receives comfort like cold porridge.°

ANTONIO. The visitor° will not give him o'er so.°

SEBASTIAN. Look, he's winding up the watch of his wit. By and by it will strike.

GONZALO. [*To* ALONSO.] Sir—

15 **SEBASTIAN.** [*To* ANTONIO.] One: tell°

GONZALO. [*To* ALONSO.] When every grief is entertained° that's offered,

---

3 **hint** occasion

9–10 **peace . . . porridge** pun on Alonzo's cry for "peace," refers to "pease porridge."

11 **visitor** one who comforts the sick in their homes;
give him o'er so leave him alone

15 **One: tell** It has struck one—keep count

16 **entertained** held in the mind

Comes to th'entertainer—

SEBASTIAN. A dollar.

GONZALO. Dolour° comes to him indeed. You have spoken truer
20 than you purposed.

SEBASTIAN. You have taken it wiselier than I meant you should.

GONZALO. [*To* ALONSO.] Therefore my lord—

ANTONIO. [*To* SEBASTIAN.] Fie, what a spendthrift is he of his tongue!

ALONSO. [*To* GONZALO.] I prithee, spare.°

25 **GONZALO.** Well, I have done. But yet—

SEBASTIAN. [*To* ANTONIO.] He will be talking.

ANTONIO. Which of he or Adrian, for a good wager, first begins
to crow?

SEBASTIAN. The old cock.

30 **ANTONIO.** The cockerel.

SEBASTIAN. Done. The wager?

ANTONIO. A laughter.°

SEBASTIAN. A match!

ADRIAN. [*To* GONZALO.] Though this island seem to be desert°—

35 **ANTONIO.** [*To* SEBASTIAN.] Ha, ha, ha!

SEBASTIAN. So, you're paid.

ADRIAN. Uninhabitable, and almost inaccessible—

SEBASTIAN. [*To* ANTONIO.] Yet—

ADRIAN. Yet—

40 **ANTONIO.** [*To* SEBASTIAN.] He could not miss't.

ADRIAN. It must needs be of subtle, tender, and delicate
temperance.°

ANTONIO. [*To* SEBASTIAN.] Temperance was a delicate wench.

SEBASTIAN. Ay, and a subtle, as he most learnedly delivered.

---

19 **Dolour** grief

24 **spare** spare your words

32 **A laughter** Reference to the saying "He laughs that wins."

34 **desert** uninhabited

42 **temperance** climate (In the next line, Antonio puns on its use as a woman's name.)

45 **ADRIAN.** [*To* GONZALO.] The air breathes upon us here most sweetly.

SEBASTIAN. [*To* ANTONIO.] As if it had lungs, and rotten ones.

ANTONIO. Or as 'twere perfumed by a fen.

GONZALO. [*To* ADRIAN] Here is everything advantageous to life.

50 **ANTONIO.** [*To* SEBASTIAN.] True, save° means to live.

SEBASTIAN. Of that there's none, or little.

GONZALO. [*To* ADRIAN.] How lush and lusty the grass looks! How green!

ANTONIO. The ground indeed is tawny.°

55 **SEBASTIAN.** With an eye° of green in't.

ANTONIO. He misses not much.

SEBASTIAN. No, he doth but mistake the truth totally.

GONZALO. [*To* ADRIAN.] But the rarity of it is, which is indeed almost beyond credit—

60 **SEBASTIAN.** [*To* ANTONIO.] As many vouched rarities° are.

GONZALO. [*To* ADRIAN.] That our garments being, as they were, drenched in the sea, hold notwithstanding their freshness and glosses, being rather new-dyed than stained with salt water.

ANTONIO. [*To* SEBASTIAN.] If but one of his pockets could speak,
65 would it not say he lies?

SEBASTIAN. Ay, or very falsely pocket up° his report.

GONZALO. [*To* ADRIAN.] Methinks our garments are now as fresh as when we put them on first in Afric,° at the marriage of the King's fair daughter Claribel to the King of Tunis.

70 **SEBASTIAN.** 'Twas a sweet marriage, and we prosper well in our return.

ADRIAN. Tunis was never graced before with such a paragon to their queen.

---

50 **save** except for

54 **tawny** yellowish-brown; parched by the sun

55 **eye** tinge

60 **vouched rarities** alleged wonders

66 **pocket up** conceal; suppress

68 **Afric** Africa

GONZALO. Not since widow Dido's° time.

75 ANTONIO. [*To SEBASTIAN.*] Widow? A pox o'that! How came that 'widow' in? Widow Dido!

SEBASTIAN. What if he had said 'widower Aeneas' too? Good Lord, how you take it!

ADRIAN. [*To GONZALO.*] 'Widow Dido' said you? You make me
80 study of that: she was of Carthage, not of Tunis.

GONZALO. This Tunis, sir, was Carthage.°

ADRIAN. Carthage?

GONZALO. I assure you, Carthage.

ANTONIO. [*To SEBASTIAN.*] His word is more than the miraculous
85 harp.°

SEBASTIAN. He hath raised the wall, and houses too.

ANTONIO. What impossible matter will he make easy next?

SEBASTIAN. I think he will carry this island home in his pocket, and give it his son for an apple.

90 ANTONIO. And sowing the kernels of it in the sea, bring forth more islands.

GONZALO. [*To ADRIAN.*] Ay.

ANTONIO. [*To SEBASTIAN.*] Why, in good time.

GONZALO. [*To ALONSO.*] Sir, we were talking that our garments
95 seem now as fresh as when we were at Tunis, at the marriage of your daughter, who is now queen.

ANTONIO. And the rarest that e'er came there.

SEBASTIAN. Bate,° I beseech you, widow Dido.

ANTONIO. O, widow Dido? Ay, widow Dido.

100 GONZALO. [*To ALONSO.*] Is not, sir, my doublet as fresh as the first day I wore it? I mean in a sort.°

ANTONIO. [*To SEBASTIAN.*] That 'sort' was well fished for.

---

74 **Dido** In Virgil's *Aeneid,* Dido is a Carthagian queen who kills herself.

81 Tunis is located near the site of Carthage, which was destroyed by the Romans.

84–85 **miraculous harp** In Greek mythology, Amphion used his harp to build a wall around Thebes.

98 **Bate** except

101 **in a sort** to some degree (In the next line, Antonio plays on the association between *sort* and the game of drawing lots.)

GONZALO. [*To* ALONSO.] When I wore it at your daughter's marriage.

105 **ALONSO.** You cram these words into mine ears against
The stomach of my sense.° Would I had never
Married my daughter there! For coming thence,
My son is lost; and, in my rate,° she too,
Who is so far from Italy removed
110 I ne'er again shall see her. O thou mine heir
Of Naples and Milan, what strange fish
Hath made his meal on thee?

FRANCISCO. Sir, he may live.
I saw him beat the surges under him
And ride upon their backs. He trod the water,
115 Whose enmity he flung aside, and breasted
The surge, most swoll'n, that met him. His bold head
'Bove the contentious waves he kept, and oared
Himself with his good arms in lusty° stroke
To th' shore, that o'er his wave-worn basis bowed,
120 As stooping to relieve him. I not doubt
He came alive to land.

ALONSO. No, no; he's gone.

SEBASTIAN. [*To* ALONSO.] Sir, you may thank yourself for this great loss,
That would not bless our Europe with your daughter,
But rather loose her to an African,
125 Where she, at least, is banished from your eye,
Who hath cause to wet the grief° on't.

ALONSO. Prithee, peace.

SEBASTIAN. You were kneeled to and importuned otherwise
By all of us, and the fair soul herself
Weighed between loathness and obedience at
130 Which end o'th' beam should bow. We have lost your son,
I fear, for ever. Milan and Naples have
More widows in them of this business' making

105-106 **against . . . sense** though I am in no mood to hear them
108 **rate** opinion
118 **lusty** vigorous
126 **wet the grief** weep

Than we bring men to comfort them. The fault's your own.

ALONSO. So is the dear'st o'th' loss.

GONZALO. My lord Sebastian,

135 The truth you speak doth lack some gentleness
And time to speak it in. You rub the sore
When you should bring the plaster.°

SEBASTIAN. [*To* ANTONIO.] Very well.

ANTONIO. And most chirurgeonly.°

140 **GONZALO.** [*To* ALONSO.] It is foul weather in us all, good sir,
When you are cloudy.

SEBASTIAN. [*To* ANTONIO.] Fowl weather?

ANTONIO. Very foul.

GONZALO. [*To* ALONSO.] Had I plantation° of this isle, my lord—

ANTONIO. [*To* SEBASTIAN.] He'd sow't with nettle-seed.

SEBASTIAN. Or docks,
or mallows.°

GONZALO. And were the king on't, what would I do?

145 **SEBASTIAN.** [*To* ANTONIO.] Scape being drunk, for want of wine.

GONZALO. I'th' commonwealth I would by contraries
Execute all things.° For no kind of traffic°
Would I admit, no name of magistrate;
Letters° should not be known; riches, poverty,
150 And use of service,° none; contract, succession,°
Bourn,° bound of land, tilth,° vineyard, none;
No use of metal, corn, or wine, or oil;
No occupation, all men idle, all;

---

137 **plaster** a healing mixture applied to the body

139 **chirurgeonly** like a surgeon

142 **plantation** colonization (In the next line, Antonio plays with the meaning "planting.")

143 **nettle-seed, docks, mallows** types of weeds

146–147 **by contraries . . . things** carry out everything in a manner opposite to what is normally done

147 **traffic** commerce

149 **Letters** writing, learning

150 **use of service** employment of servants;
succession inheritance

151 **Bourn** boundary;
tilth raising crops

And women too—but innocent and pure;
155 No sovereignty—

SEBASTIAN. [*To ANTONIO.*] Yet he would be king on't.

ANTONIO. The latter end of his commonwealth forgets the beginning.

GONZALO. [*To ALONSO.*] All things in common° nature should produce
Without sweat or endeavour. Treason, felony,
160 Sword, pike, knife, gun, or need of any engine,°
Would I not have; but nature should bring forth
Of it° own kind all foison,° all abundance,
To feed my innocent people.

SEBASTIAN. [*To ANTONIO.*] No marrying 'mong his subjects?

165 **ANTONIO.** None, man, all idle: whores and knaves.

GONZALO. [*To ALONSO.*] I would with such perfection govern, sir,
T'excel the Golden Age.

SEBASTIAN. Save° his majesty!

ANTONIO. Long live Gonzalo!

GONZALO. [*To ALONSO.*] And—do you mark me, sir?

ALONSO. Prithee, no more. Thou dost talk nothing to me.

170 **GONZALO.** I do well believe your highness, and did it to minister occasion° to these gentlemen, who are of such sensible° and nimble lungs that they always use to laugh at nothing.

ANTONIO. 'Twas you we laughted at.

GONZALO. Who, in this kind of merry fooling, am nothing to you.
170 So you may continue, and laugh at nothing still.

ANTONIO. What a blow was there given!

SEBASTIAN. An it had not fallen flat-long.°

---

157 **in common** for communal use

160 **engine** weapon

162 **it** its;
foison plenty

167 **Save** God save

170–171 **minister occasion** furnish an opportunity

171 **sensible** sensitive

178 **flat-long** from the flat side of the sword (rather than the edge)

GONZALO. You are a gentlemen of brave mettle. You would lift the moon out of her sphere, if she would continue in it five
180 weeks without changing.

[*Enter* ARIEL, *invisible, playing solemn music.*]

SEBASTIAN. We would so, and then go a-bat-fowling.°

ANTONIO. [*To* GONZALO.] Nay, good my lord, be not angry.

GONZALO. No, I warrant you, I will not adventure my discretion so weakly.° Will you laugh me asleep? For I am very heavy.

185 **ANTONIO.** Go sleep, and hear us.

[GONZALO, ADRIAN, *and* FRANCISCO *sleep.*]

ALONSO. What, all so soon asleep? I wish mine eyes
Would, with themselves, shut up my thoughts.—I find
They are inclined to do so.

SEBASTIAN. Please you, sir,
Do not omit the heavy offer of it.
190 I seldom visits sorrow; when it doth,
It is a comforter.

ANTONIO. We two, my lord,
Will guard your person while you take your rest,
And watch your safety.

ALONSO. Thank you. Wondrous heavy.

[*He sleeps. Exit* ARIEL.]

SEBASTIAN. What a strange drowsiness possesses them!

195 **ANTONIO.** It is the quality o'th' climate.

SEBASTIAN. Why
Doth it not then our eyelids sink? I find
Not myself disposed to sleep.

ANTONIO. Nor I; my spirits are nimble.
They fell together all, as by consent;
They dropped as by a thunderstroke. What might,
200 Worthy Sebastian, O, what might—? No more!—
And yet methinks I see it in thy face.
What thou shouldst be th'occasion speaks thee° and

---

181 **bat-fowling** attracting night birds with a light, then striking them down with a bat

183–184 **adventure . . . weakly** risk my reputation by behaving so weakly

202 **What thou . . . thee** The opportunity reveals to you what you should be.

My strong imagination sees a crown
Dropping upon thy head.

SEBASTIAN. What, art thou waking?

205 **ANTONIO.** Do you not hear me speak?

SEBASTIAN. I do, and surely
It is a sleepy language, and thou speak'st
Out of thy sleep. What is it thou didst say?
This is a strange repose, to be asleep
With eyes wide open; standing, speaking, moving,
210 And yet so fast asleep.

ANTONIO. Noble Sebastian,
Thou letst thy fortune sleep, die rather; wink'st°
Whiles thou art waking.

SEBASTIAN. Thou dost snore distinctly;
There's meaning in thy snores.

ANTONIO. I am more serious than my custom. You
215 Must be so too if heed me, which to do
Trebles thee o'er.°

SEBASTIAN. Well, I am standing water.°

ANTONIO. I'll teach you how to flow.

SEBASTAIN. Do so; to ebb
Hereditary sloth° instructs me.

ANTONIO. O,
If you but knew how you the purpose cherish°
220 Whiles thus you mock it; how in stripping it
You more invest it! Ebbing° men, indeed,
Most often do so near the bottom run
By their own fear or sloth.

SEBASTIAN. Prithee, say on.
The setting° of thine eye and cheek proclaim

---

211 **wink'st** you close your eyes

216 **Trebles thee o'er** makes you three times as great;
standing water neither ebbing nor flowing (he waits to hear what Antonio has to say)

217–218 **to ebb . . . sloth** My natural laziness or status as a younger brother

219 **If you . . . cherish** If only you realized how you encourage the intention

221 **Ebbing** unsuccessful

224 **setting** fixed look

225 A matter° from thee, and a birth, indeed,
Which throes thee much to yield.°

ANTONIO. Thus, sir.
Although this lord of weak remembrance, this,
Who shall be of as little memory°
When he is earthed,° hath here almost persuaded—
230 For he's a spirit of persuasion, only
Professes to persuade°—the King his son's alive,
'Tis as impossible that he's undrowned
As he that sleeps here swims.

SEBASTIAN. I have no hope
That he's undrowned.

ANTONIO. O, out of that 'no hope'
235 What great hope have you! No hope that way° is
Another way so high a hope that even
Ambition cannot pierce a wink beyond,
But doubt discovery there.° Will you grant with me
That Ferdinand is drowned?

SEBASTIAN. He's gone.

ANTONIO. Then tell me,
240 Who's the next heir of Naples?

SEBASTIAN. Claribel.

ANTONIO. She that is Queen of Tunis; she that dwells
Ten leagues beyond man's life;° she that from Naples
Can have no note°—unless the sun were post°
The man i'th' moon's too slow—till new-born chins
245 Be rough and razorable;° she that from whom

---

225 **a matter** something important
226 **throes thee much to yield** causes you great pain to bring forth (as in childbirth)
228 **of as little memory** as quickly forgotten
229 **earthed** buried
230–231 **only . . . persuade** his only profession is to persuade
235 **that way** that Ferdinand hasn't drowned
237–238 **cannot pierce . . . there** cannot set its sight on anything greater
242 **beyond man's life** farther than one can travel in a lifetime
243 **note** information;
post messenger
244–245 **till new-born . . . razorable** until enough time passed for a baby boy to become old enough to shave

We all were sea-swallowed, though some cast again°—
And by that destiny, to perform an act
Whereof what's past is prologue, what to come
In yours and my discharge.°

SEBASTIAN. What stuff is this? How say you?
250 'Tis true my brother's daughter's Queen of Tunis;
So is she heir of Naples; 'twixt which regions
There is some space.

ANTONIO. A space whose every cubit°
Seems to cry out 'How shall that Claribel
Measure us° back to Naples? Keep in Tunis,
255 And let Sebastian wake.' Say this were death
That now hath seized them;° why, they were no worse
Than now they are. There be that can rule Naples
As well as he that sleeps, lords that can prate°
As amply and unnecessarily
260 As this Gonzalo; I myself could make
A chough of as deep chat.° O, that you bore
The mind that I do, what a sleep were this
For your advancement! Do you understand me?

SEBASTIAN. Methinks I do.

ANTONIO. And how does your content
265 Tender° your own good fortune?

SEBASTIAN. I remember
You did supplant your brother Prospero.

ANTONIO. True;
And look how well my garments sit upon me,
Much feater° than before. My brother's servants
Were then my fellows; now they are my men.

270 **SEBASTIAN.** But for your conscience.

---

246 **cast again** cast ashore or cast into new roles
249 **discharge** performance
252 **cubit** seventeen to twenty-two inches
254 **Measure us** travel over our length
256 **them** Alonso and Gonzalo (who are sleeping)
258 **prate** babble
260 **make . . . chat** train a jackdaw (a bird related to the crow) to talk as profoundly as he does
264–265 **how does . . . Tender** what do you think of
268 **feater** more suitably

ANTONIO. Ay, sir, where lies that? If 'twere a kibe
'Twould put me to my slipper°; but I feel not
This deity in my bosom. Twenty consciences
That stand 'twixt me and Milan, candied be they,
275 And melt° ere they molest. Here lies your brother,
No better than the earth he lies upon
If he were that which now he's like—that's dead;
Whom I with this obedient steel,° three inches of it,
Can lay to bed for ever; whiles you, doing thus,
280 To the perpetual wink for aye might put°
This ancient morsel, this Sir Prudence, who
Should not upbraid our course. For all the rest,
They'll take suggestion as a cat laps milk;
They'll tell the clock to any business that
285 We say befits the hour.°

SEBASTIAN. Thy case, dear friend,
Shall be my precedent. As thou got'st Milan,
I'll come by Naples. Draw thy sword. One stroke
Shall free thee from the tribute which thou payest,
And I the King shall love thee.

ANTONIO. Draw together,
290 And when I rear my hand, do you the like
To fall it on Gonzalo.

[*They draw.*]

SEBASTIAN. O, but one word.

[*Enter* ARIEL, *invisible, with music and song.*]

ARIEL. [*To* GONZALO.] My master through his art forsees the danger
That you his friend are in—and sends me forth,
For else° his project dies, to keep them° living.

[*He sings in* GONZALO*'s ear.*]

271–272 **If 'twere . . . slipper** If it were a sore on my heel, it would force me to put on slippers
275 **melt** dissolved
278 **steel** sword
280 **To the . . . put** might put to sleep forever
284–285 **tell the . . . hour** agree to anything that we say is appropriate
294 **else** otherwise;
them Gonzalo and Alonso

295 While you here do snoring lie,
Open-eyed conspiracy
His time doth take.
If of life you keep a care,
Shake off slumber, and beware.
300 Awake, awake!

ANTONIO. [*To* SEBASTIAN.] Then let us both be sudden.

GONZALO. [*Awaking.*] Now good angels
Perserve the King!

ALONSO. [*Awaking.*] Why, how now? Ho, awake!

[*The others awake.*]

[*To* ANTONIO *and* SEBASTIAN.] Why are you drawn?°
[*To* GONZALO.] Wherefore this ghastly looking?

GONZALO. What's the matter?

305 **SEBASTIAN.** Whiles we stood here securing your repose,°
Even now we heard a hollow burst of bellowing,
Like bulls, or rather lions. Did't not wake you?
It struck mine ear most terribly.

ALONSO. I heard nothing.

ANTONIO. O, 'twas a din to fright a monster's ear,
310 To make an earthquake! Sure it was the roar
Of a whole herd of lions.

ALONSO. Heard you this, Gonzalo?

GONZALO. Upon mine honour, sir, I heard a humming,
And that a strange one too, which did awake me.
I shaked you, sir, and cried.° As mine eyes opened.
315 I saw their weapons drawn. There was a noise,
That's verily.° 'Tis best we stand upon our guard,
Or that we quit this place. Let's draw our weapons.

ALONSO. Lead off this ground, and let's make further search
For my poor son.

---

303 **Why are you drawn** Why have you drawn your weapons?

305 **securing your respose** guarding your sleep

314 **cried** cried out

316 **verily** true

GONZALO. Heavens keep him from these beasts!
320 For he is sure i'th' island.

ALONSO. Lead away.

[*Exeunt all but* ARIEL.]

ARIEL. Prospero my lord shall know what I have done.
So, King, go safely on to seek thy son.

[*Exit.*]

Scene 2

[*Enter* CALIBAN, *wearing a gaberdine, and with a burden of wood.*]

CALIBAN. [*Throwing down his burden.*] All the infections that the sun sucks up
From bogs, fens, flats° on Prosper fall, and make him
By inch-meal° a disease!

[A *noise of thunder is heard.*]

His spirts hear me,
And yet I needs must curse. But they'll nor pinch,
5 Fright me with urchin-shows° pitch me i'th' mire,
Nor lead me like a fire-brand° in the dark
Out of my way, unless he bid 'em. But
For every triffle are they set upon me;
Sometime like apes, that mow° and chatter at me
10 And after bite me; then like hedgehogs, which
Lie tumbling in my barefoot way and mount
Their pricks at my footfall; sometime am I
All wound° with adders,° who with cloven tongues
Do hiss me into madness.

[*Enter* TRINCULO.]

---

2 **flats** swamps
3 **By inch-meal** inch by inch
5 **urchin-shows** goblins appearing in the shape of hedgehogs
6 **fire-brand** piece of burning wood
9 **mow** grimace
13 **wound** entwined;
adders snakes

Lo now, lo!

15 Here comes a spirit of his, and to torment me
For bringing wood in slowly. I'll fall flat.
Perchance he will not mind me.

[*He lies down.*]

TRINCULO. Here's neither bush nor shrub to bear off° any weather at all, and another storm brewing. I hear it sing i'th'
20 wind. Yon same black cloud, yon huge one, looks like a foul bombard° that would shed his liquor. If it should thunder as it did before, I know not where to hide my head. Yon same cloud cannot choose but fall by pailfuls. [*Seeing* CALIBAN.] What have we here, a man or a fish? Dead or alive?—A fish, he smells
25 like a fish; a very ancient and fish-like smell; a kind of not-of-the-newest poor-john.° A strange fish! Were I in England now, as once I was, and had but this fish painted,° not a holiday-fool there but would give a piece of silver. There would this monster make a man.° Any strange beast there makes a man. When
30 they will not give a doit° to relieve a lame beggar, they will lay out ten to see a dead Indian.° Legged like a man, and his fins like arms! Warm, o'my troth! I do now let loose my opinion, hold it no longer. This is no fish, but an islander that hath lately suffered° by a thunderbolt. [*Thunder.*] Alas, the storm
35 is come again. My best way is to creep under his gaberdine;° there is no other shelter herabout. Misery acquaints a man with strange bedfellows. I will here shroud° till the dregs of the storm be past.

[*He hides under* CALIBAN'S *gaberdine. Enter* STEFANO, *singing, with a wooden bottle in his hand.*]

---

18 **bear off** ward off
21 **bombard** large leather jug
26 **poor-john** dried fish
27 **painted** painted on a sign (to attract spectators)
29 **make a man** make a man's fortune
30 **doit** small coin
31 **dead Indian** Native Americans were popular exhibits in London.
34 **suffered** perished
36 **gaberdine** cloak
37 **shroud** take shelter

STEFANO. I shall no more to sea, to sea,
40 Here shall I die ashore—
This is a very scurvy tune to sing at a man's funeral.
Well, here's my comfort.

[*He drinks, then sings.*]

The master, the swabber,° the boatswain, and I,
The gunner and his mate,
45 Loved Mall, Meg, and Marian, and Margery,
But none of us cared for Kate.
For she had a tongue with a tang,
Would cry to a sailor 'Go hang!'
She loved not the savour of tar nor of pitch,
50 Yet a tailor might scratch her where'er she did itch.
Then to sea, boys, and let her go hang!
Then to sea [*etc.*].
This is a scurvy tune, too. But here's my comfort.

[*He drinks.*]

CALIBAN. [*To* TRINCULO.] Do not torment me! O!

55 **STEFANO.** What's the matter? Have we devils here? Do you put tricks upon's with savages and men of Ind,° ha? I have not scaped drowning to be afeard now of your four legs. For it hath been said: 'As proper a man as ever went on four legs cannot make him give ground.' And it shall be said so again, while
60 Stefano breathes at° nostrils.

CALIBAN. The spirit torments me. O!

STEFANO. This is some monster of the isle with four legs, who hath got, as I take it, an ague.° Where the devil should he learn our language? I will give him some relief, if it be but for that.
65 If I can recover° him and keep him tame and get to Naples with him, he's a present for any emperor that ever trod on neat's leather.°

---

43 **swabber** seaman who cleans the deck

55–56 **put tricks . . . Ind** try to fool us with illusions of savages and men of India

60 **at** at the

63 **ague** fever (because it is shivering)

65 **recover** cure

66–67 **neat's leather** cowhide (shoes)

CALIBAN. [*To* TRINCULO.] Do not torment me, prithee! I'll bring my wood home faster.

70 **STEFANO.** He's in his fit now, and does not talk after the wisest. He shall taste of my bottle. If he have never drunk wine afore, it will go near to remove his fit. If I can recover him and keep him tame, I will not take too much for him.° He shall pay for him that hath him, and that soundly.

75 **CALIBAN.** [*To* TRINCULO.] Thou dost me yet but little hurt. Thou wilt anon, I know it by thy trembling. Now Prosper works upon thee.

STEFANO. Come on your ways. Open your mouth. Here is that which will give language to you, cat. Open your mouth. This
80 will shake your shaking, I can tell you, and that soundly. You cannot tell who's your friend. Open your chaps again.

[CALIBAN *drinks*.]

TRINCULO. I should know that voice. It should be—but he is drowned, and these are devils. O, defend me!

STEFANO. Four legs and two voices—a most delicate° monster!
85 His forward voice now is to speak well of his friend; his backward voice is to utter foul speeches and to detract. If all the wine in my bottle will recover him, I will help his ague. Come. [CALIBAN *drinks*.] Amen. I will pour some in thy other mouth.

90 **TRINCULO.** Stefano!

STEFANO. Doth thy other mouth call me? Mercy, mercy! This is a devil, and no monster. I will leave him. I have no long spoon.°

TRINCULO. Stefano! If thou beest Stefano, touch me and speak
95 to me, for I am Trinculo. Be not afeard. Thy good friend Trinculo.

STEFANO. If thou beest Trinculo, come forth. I'll pull thee by the lesser legs. If any be Trinculo's legs, these are they.

[*He pulls out* TRINCULO *by the legs*.]

---

73 **I will . . . him** No price could be too high for him.

84 **delicate** exquisitely made

92–93 Allusion to the saying "He must have a long spoon that will eat with the devil."

Thou are very Trinculo indeed! How cam'st thou to be the
100 siege° of this moon-calf?° Can he vent° Trinculos?

TRINCULO. [*Rising.*] I took him to be killed with a thunderstroke. But are thou not drowned, Stefano? I hope now thou art not drowned. Is the storm overblown? I hid me under the dead moon-calf's gaberdine for fear of the storm. And art thou living,
105 Stefano? O Stefano, two Neapolitans scaped!

[*He dances* STEFANO *round.*]

STEFANO. Prithee, do not turn me about. My stomach is not constant.

CALIBAN. These be fine things, an if° they be not spirits.
That's a brave° god, and bears celestial liquor.
110 I will kneel to him.

[*He kneels.*]

STEFANO. [*To* TRINCULO.] How didst thou scape? How cam'st thou hither? Swear by this bottle how thou cam'st hither. I escaped upon a butt of sack° which the sailors heaved o'erboard, by this bottle—which I made of the bark of a tree with mine own
115 hands since I was cast ashore.

CALIBAN. I'll swear upon that bottle to by thy true subject, for the liquor is not earthly.

STEFANO. [*Offering* TRINCULO *the bottle.*] Here. Swear then how thou escapedst.

120 **TRINCULO.** Swum ashore, man, like a duck. I can swim like a duck, I'll be sworn.

STEFANO. Here, kiss the book.°

[TRINCULO *drinks.*]

Though thou canst swim like a duck, thou art made like a goose.

---

100 **siege** excrement;
moon-calf monstrosity;
vent excrete

108 **an if** if

109 **brave** fine

113 **butt of sack** barrel of wine

122 **kiss the book** a parody of kissing the Bible to confirm an oath

125 **TRINCULO.** O Stefano, hast any more of this?

STEFANO. The whole butt, man. My cellar is in a rock by th' seaside, where my wine is hid. [*CALIBAN rises.*] How now, moon-calf? How does thine ague?

CALIBAN. Hast thou not dropped from heaven?

130 **STEFANO.** Out o'th' moon, I do assure thee. I was the man i'th' moon when time was.°

CALIBAN. I have seen thee in her, and I do adore thee.
My mistress showed me thee, and thy dog and thy bush.

STEFANO. Come, swear to that. Kiss the book. I will furnish it
135 anon with new contents. Swear.

[*Caliban drinks.*]

TRINCULO. By this good light,° this is a very shallow monster! I afeard of him? A very weak monster! The man i'th' moon? A most poor, credulous monster! Well drawn,° monster, in good sooth°!

140 **CALIBAN.** [*To STEFANO.*] I'll show thee every fertile inch o'th' island,
And I will kiss thy foot. I prithee, be my god.

TRINCULO. By this light, a most perfidious and drunken monster! When's god's asleep, he'll rob his bottle.

145 **CALIBAN.** [*To STEFANO.*] I'll kiss thy foot. I'll swear myself thy subject.

STEFANO. Come on then; down, and swear.

[*CALIBAN kneels.*]

TRINCULO. I shall laugh myself to death at this puppy-headed monster. A most scurvy monster! I could find in my heart to
150 beat him—

STEFANO. [*To CALIBAN.*] Come, kiss.

[*CALIBAN kisses his foot.*]

---

131 when time was once upon a time
136 this good light the sun
138 drawn drunk
139 sooth truth

TRINCULO. But that the poor monster's in drink.° An abominable monster!

CALIBAN. I'll show thee the best springs; I'll pluck thee berries;
155 I'll fish for thee, and get thee wood enough.
A plague upon the tyrant that I serve!
I'll bear him no more sticks, but follow thee,
Thou wondrous man.

TRINCULO. A most ridiculous monster, to make a wonder of a poor
160 drunkard!

CALIBAN. [*To* STEFANO.] I prithee, let me bring thee where crabs grow,
And I with my long nails will dig thee pig-nuts,°
Show thee a jay's nest, and instruct thee how
To snare the nimble marmoset.° I'll bring thee
165 To clust'ring filberts, and sometimes I'll get thee
Young seamews° from the rock. Wilt thou go with me?

STEFANO. I prithee now, lead the way without any more talking.—Trinculo, the King and all our company else being drowned, we will inherit here.—Here, bear my bottle.—Fel-
170 low Trinculo, we'll fill him by and by again.

CALIBAN. [*Sings drunkenly.*] Farewell, master, farewell, farewell!

TRINCULO. A howling monster, a drunken monster!

CALIBAN. [*Sings.*] No more dams I'll make for° fish,
Nor fetch in firing°
175 At requiring,
Nor scrape trenchering,° nor wash dish.
'Ban, 'ban, Cacaliban
Has a new master.—Get a new man!
Freedom, high-day!° High-day, freedom! Freedom, high-day,
180 freedom!

STEFANO. O brave monster! Lead the way. [*Exeunt.*]

---

152 **in drink** drunk
162 **pig-nuts** edible roots
164 **marmoset** a small monkey
166 **seamews** seagulls
173 **for** to catch
174 **firing** firewood
176 **trenchering** wooden plates
179 **high-day** holiday

Act 3

Scene 1

[*Enter* FERDINAND, *bearing a log.*]

FERDINAND. There be some sports are painful, and their labour
Delight in them sets off.° Some kinds of baseness
Are nobly undergone, and most poor matters
Point to rich ends. This my mean° task
5 Would be as heavy to me as odious, but
The mistress which I serve quickens° what's dead,
And makes my labours pleasures. O, she is
Ten times more gentle than her father's crabbed,
And he's composed of harshness. I must remove
10 Some thousands of these logs and pile them up,
Upon a sore injunction.° My sweet mistress
Weeps when she sees me work, and says such baseness
Had never like executor.° I forget,
But these sweet thoughts do even refresh my labours,
15 Most busil'est when I do it.

[*Enter* MIRANDA, *and* PROSPERO *following at a distance.*]

MIRANDA. Alas now, pray you
Work not so hard. I would the lightning had
Burnt up those logs that you are enjoined to pile.
Pray set it down, and rest you. When this burns
'Twill weep for having wearied you. My father

1–2 **their labour . . . sets off** Their delights offset their painful aspects.
4 **mean** lowly
6 **quickens** revives
11 **sore injunction** harsh command
12–13 **such baseness . . . executor** Such lowly work was never done by one so noble.

20 Is hard at study. Pray now, rest yourself.
He's safe° for these three hours.

FERDINAND. O most dear mistress,
The sun will set before I shall discharge
What I must strive to do.

MIRANDA. If you'll sit down
I'll bear your logs the while. Pray give me that;
25 I'll carry it to the pile.

FERDINAND. No precious creature.
I had rather crack my sinews, break my back,
Than you should such dishonour undergo
While I sit lazy by.

MIRANDA. It would become me
As well as it does you; and I should do it
30 With much more ease, for my good will is to it,
And yours it is against.

PROSPERO. [*Aside.*] Poor worm,° thou art infected.°
This visitation shows it.

MIRANDA. [*To* FERDINAND.] You look wearily.

FERDINAND. No, noble mistress, 'tis fresh morning with me
When you are by at night. I do beseech you,
35 Chiefly that I might set it in my prayers,
What is your name?

MIRANDA. Miranda, O my father,
I have broke your hest° to say so!

FERDINAND. Admired Miranda!
Indeed the top of admiration, worth
What's dearest to the world. Full many a lady
40 I have eyed with best regard, and many a time
Th' harmony of their tongues hath into bondage
Brought my too diligent° ear. For several° virtues
Have I liked several women; never any

---

21 **safe** unable to harm us

31 **worm** used here as a term of endearment;
infected lovesick

37 **hest** command

42 **diligent** attentive;
several different; various

With so full soul but some defect in her
45 Did quarrel with the noblest grace she owed
And put it to the foil. But you, O you,
So perfect and so peerless, are created
Of every creature's best.

MIRANDA. I do not know
One of my sex, no woman's face remember
50 Save from my glass° mine own; nor have I seen
More that I may call men than you, good friend,
And my dear father. How features are abroad
I am skilless of;° but, by my modesty,
The jewel in my dower,° I would not wish
55 Any companion in the world but you;
Nor can imagination form a shape
Besides yourself to like of. But I prattle
Something too wildly, and my father's precepts°
I therein do forget.

FERDINAND. I am in my condition°
60 A prince, Miranda, I do think a king—
I would not so—and would no more endure
This wooden slavery° than to suffer
The flesh-fly° blow° my mouth. Hear my soul speak.
The very instant that I saw you did
65 My heart fly to your service; there resides
To make me slave to it. And for your sake
Am I this patient log-man.

MIRANDA. Do you love me?

FERDINAND. O heaven, O earth, bear witness to this sound,
And crown what I profess with kind event
70 If I speak true! If hollowly, invert
What best is boded me to mischief!° I,

---

50 **glass** mirror

52–53 **How features . . . of** I don't know what people look like elsewhere

54 **jewel in my dower** my most precious possession

58 **precepts** orders

59 **condition** social position

62 **wooden slavery** carrying logs

63 **flesh-fly** an insect that deposits eggs in flesh; **blow** deposit eggs in

70–71 **If hollowly . . . mischief** If I lie, turn all my good luck into bad.

Beyond all limit of what else i' th' world,
Do love, prize, honour you.

MIRANDA. [*Weeping.*] I am a fool
To weep at what I am glad of.

PROSPERO. [*Aside.*] Fair encounter
75 Of two most rare affections! Heavens rain grace
On that which breeds between 'em.

FERDINAND. [*To* MIRANDA.] Wherefore° weep you?

MIRANDA. At mine unworthiness, that dare not offer
What I desire to give, and much less take
What I shall die to want.° But this is trifling,
80 And all the more it seeks to hide itself
The bigger bulk it shows. Hence, bashful cunning,
And prompt me, plain and holy innocence.
I am your wife, if you will marry me.
If not, I'll die your maid. To be your fellow°
85 You may deny me, but I'll be your servant
Whether you will or no.

FERDINAND. [*Kneeling.*] My mistress,° dearest;
And I thus humble ever.

MIRANDA. My husband then?

FERDINAND. Ay, with a heart as willing
90 As bondage e'er of freedom.° Here's my hand.

MIRANDA. And mine, with my heart in't. And now farewell
Till half an hour hence.

FERDINAND. A thousand thousand.°

[*Exeunt severally* MIRANDA *and* FERDINAND.]

PROSPERO. So glad of this as they I cannot be,
Who are surprised with all; but my rejoicing
95 At nothing can be more. I'll to my book,°

---

76 **Wherefore** why
79 **to want** from lacking
84 **fellow** companion or equal
86 **mistress** sweetheart
89–90 **as willing . . . freedom** as desirous of it as a slave for freedom
92 **thousand thousand** million farewells
95 **book** book of magic

For yet ere supper-time must I perform
Much business appertaining.°

[*Exit.*]

Scene 2

[*Enter* CALIBAN, STEFANO, *and* TRINCULO.]

STEFANO [*To* CALIBAN.] Tell not me. When the butt is out° we will drink water, not a drop before. Therefore bear up and board 'em.° Servant monster, drink to me.

TRINCULO. Servant monster? The folly of this island! They say
5 there's but five upon this isle. We are three of them; if th'other two be brained like us,° the state totters.

STEFANO. Drink, servant monster, when I bid thee. Thy eyes are almost set° in thy head.

TRINCULO. Where should they be set else? He were a brave
10 monster indeed if they were set in his tail.

STEFANO. My man-monster hath drowned his tongue in sack. For my part, the sea cannot drown me. I swam, ere I could recover the shore, five and thirty leagues,° off and on. By this light, thou shalt be my lieutenant, monster, or my standard.°

15 **TRINCULO.** Your lieutenant if you list;° he's no standard.

STEFANO. We'll not run, Monsieur Monster.

TRINCULO. Nor go neither; but you'll lie like dogs, and yet say nothing neither.

STEFANO. Moon-calf, speak once in thy life, if thou beest a good
20 moon-calf.

CALIBAN. How does thy honour? Let me lick thy shoe.
I'll not serve him; he is not valiant.

---

97 **appertaining** relating to this
1 **butt is out** barrel of wine is empty
2–3 **bear up and board 'em** drink up
6 **be brained like us** have brains like ours
8 **set** fixed (from drunkenness)
13 **five and thirty leagues** about a hundred miles
14 **standard** standard-bearer
15 **list** wish

TRINCULO. Thou liest, most ignorant monster! I am in case° to jostle a constable. Why, thou debauched fish, thou, was there
25 ever man a coward that hath drunk so much sack as I today? Wilt thou tell a monstrous lie, being but half a fish and half a monster?

CALIBAN. [*To* STEFANO.] Lo, how he mocks me! Wilt thou let him, my lord?

30 **TRINCULO.** 'Lord' quoth he? That a monster should be such a natural!°

CALIBAN. [*To* STEFANO.] Lo, lo, again! Bite him to death, I prithee.

STEFANO. Trinculo, keep a good tongue in your head. If you prove a mutineer, the next tree.° The poor monster's my sub-
35 ject, and he shall not suffer indignity.

CALIBAN. I thank my noble lord. Wilt thou be pleased
To hearken once again to the suit° I made to thee?

STEFANO. Marry,° will I. Kneel and repeat it. I will stand, and so shall Trinculo.

[CALIBAN *kneels. Enter* ARIEL, *invisible.*]

40 **CALIBAN.** As I told thee before, I am subject to a tyrant, a sorcerer, that by his cunning hath cheated me of the island.

ARIEL. Thou liest.

CALIBAN. [*To* TRINCULO.] Thou liest, thou jesting monkey, thou.
I would my valiant master would destroy thee.
45 I do not lie.

STEFANO. Trinculo, if you trouble him any more in's tale, by this hand, I will supplant some of your teeth.

TRINCULO. Why, I said nothing.

STEFANO. Mum, then, and no more. [*To* CALIBAN.] Proceed.

50 **CALIBAN.** I say by sorcery he got this isle;
From me he got it. If thy greatness will

---

23 **in case** in a condition (because he's drunk)

31 **natural** idiot (playing on the idea that monsters are unnatural)

34 **the next tree** You'll hang on the next tree.

37 **suit** petition

38 **Marry** Indeed

Revenge it on him—for I know thou dar'st,
But this thing° dare not—

STEFANO. That's most certain.

55 **CALIBAN.** Thou shall be lord of it, and I'll serve thee.

STEFANO. How now shall this be compassed?° Canst thou bring me to the party?

CALIBAN. Yea, yea, my lord. I'll yield him thee asleep
Where thou mayst knock a nail into his head.

60 **ARIEL.** Thou liest, thou canst not.

CALIBAN. What a pied ninny's° this! [*To* TRINCULO.] Thou scurvy patch.°
[*To* STEFANO.] I do beseech thy greatness give him blows,
And take his bottle from him. When that's gone
He shall drink naught but brine, for I'll not show him
65 Where the quick freshes° are.

STEFANO. Trinculo, run into no further danger. Interrupt the monster one word further, and, by this hand, I'll turn my mercy out o'doors and make a stockfish° of thee.

TRINCULO. Why, what did I? I did nothing. I'll go father off.

70 **STEFANO.** Didst thou not say he lied?

ARIEL. Thou liest.

STEFANO. Do I so? [*Striking* TRINCULO.] Take thou that. As you like this, give me the lie° another time.

TRINCULO. I did not give the lie. Out o'your wits and hearing
75 too? A pox o'your bottle! This can sack and drinking do. A murrain° on your monster, and the devil take your fingers.

CALIBAN. Ha, ha, ha!

STEFANO. Now forward with your tale. [*To* TRINCULO.] Prithee,

---

53 **this thing** Trinculo

56 **compassed** achieved

61 **pied ninny's** referring to his multicolored jester's outfit; **patch** jester

65 **quick freshes** flowing streams

68 **stockfish** dried cod that is beaten before being cooked

73 **give me the lie** call me a liar

76 **murrain** plague

stand further off.

80 **CALIBAN.** Beat him enough; after a little time
I'll beat him too.

STEFANO. [*To* TRINCULO.]
Stand farther. [*To* CALIBAN.] Come, proceed.

CALIBAN. Why, as I told thee, 'tis a custom with him
I'th' afternoon to sleep. There° thou mayst brain him,
Having first seized his books; or with a log
85 Batter his skull, or paunch him with a stake,
Or cut his weasand° with thy knife. Remember
First to possess his books, for without them
He's but a sot as I am, nor hath not
One spirit to command—they all do hate him
90 As rootedly as I. Burn but his books.
He has brave utensils,° for so he calls them,
Which when he has a house he'll deck withal.
And that most deeply to consider is
The beauty of his daughter. He himself
95 Calls her a nonpareil.° I never saw a woman
But only Sycorax my dam and she,
But she as far surpasseth Sycorax
As great'st does least.

STEFANO. Is it so brave° a lass?

CALIBAN. Ay, lord. She will become thy bed, I warrant,
100 And bring thee forth brave brood.

STEFANO. Monster, I will kill this man. His daughter and I will be king and queen—save° our graces!—and Trinculo and thyself shall be viceroys. Dost thou like the plot, Trinculo?

TRINCULO. Excellent.

105 **STEFANO.** Give me thy hand. I am sorry I beat thee. But while thou liv'st, keep a good tongue in thy head.

CALIBAN. Within this half hour will he be asleep.

---

83 **There** then

86 **weasand** throat

91 **utensils** household goods

95 **nonpareil** person without equal

98 **brave** fine

102 **save** God save

Wilt thou destroy him then?

STEFANO. Ay, on mine honour.

110 **ARIEL.** [*Aside.*] This will I tell my master.

CALIBAN. Thou mak'st me merry; I am full of pleasure.
Let us be jocund. Will you troll the catch°
You taught me but while-ere?°

STEFANO. At thy request, monster, I will do reason, any rea-
115 son°—Come on, Trinculo, let us sing.

[*Sings.*] Flout 'em and cout° 'em,
And scout° 'em and flout 'em.
Thought is free.

CALIBAN. That's not the tune.

[ARIEL *plays the tune on a tabor° and pipe.*]

120 **STEFANO.** What is this same?

TRINCULO. This is the tune of our catch, played by the picture of Nobody.

STEFANO. [*Calls towards* ARIEL.] If thou beest a man, show thyself in thy likeness. If thou beest a devil, take't as thou list.

125 **TRINCULO.** O, forgive me my sins!

STEFANO. He that dies pays all debts. [*Calls.*] I defy thee.—
Mercy upon us!

CALIBAN. Art thou afeared?

STEFANO. No, monster, not I.

130 **CALIBAN.** Be not afeared. The isle is full of noises,
Sounds, and sweet airs, that give delight and hurt not.
Sometimes a thousand twangling instruments
Will hum about mine ears, and sometimes voices
That if I then had waked after long sleep
135 Will make me sleep again; and then in dreaming
The clouds methought would open and show riches

---

112 **troll the catch** sing the song

113 **but while-ere** just a while ago

114–115 **any reason** anything reasonable

116 **cout** cheat

117 **scout** mock

119 **tabor** small drum

Ready to drop upon me, that when I waked
I cried to dream again.

STEFANO. This will prove a brave kingdom to me, where I shall
140 have my music for nothing.

CALIBAN. When Prospero is destroyed.

STEFANO. That shall be by and by. I remember the story.

[*Exit* ARIEL, *playing music*.]

TRINCULO. The sound is going away. Let's follow it, and after do our work.

145 **STEFANO.** Lead, monster; we'll follow.—I would I could see this taborer. He lays it on.°

TRINCULO. [*To* CALIBAN.] Wilt come? I'll follow Stefano.

[*Exeunt*.]

Scene 3

[*Enter* ALONSO, SEBASTIAN, ANTONIO, GONZALO, ADRIAN, *and* FRANCISCO.]

GONZALO. [*To* ALONSO.] By'r la'kin, I can go no further, sir.
My old bones ache. Here's a maze trod indeed
Through forthrights and meanders.° By your patience,
I needs must rest me.

ALONSO. Old lord, I cannot blame thee,
5 Who am myself attached with weariness
To th' dulling of my spirits. Sit down and rest.
Even here I will put off my hope, and keep it
No longer for my flatterer. He is drowned
Whom thus we stray to find, and the sea mocks
10 Our frustrate search on land. Well, let him go.

[*They sit*.]

ANTONIO. [*Aside to* SEBASTIAN.] I am right glad that he's so out of hope.
Do not for one repulse° forgo the purpose
That you resolved t'effect.

---

146 **lays it on** plays vigorously
3 **forthrights and meanders** straight and winding paths
12 **for one repulse** because of one setback

SEBASTIAN. [*Aside to* ANTONIO.] The next advantage°
Will we take throughly.°

ANTONIO. [*Aside to* SEBASTIAN.] Let it be tonight,
15 For now they are oppressed with travel. They
Will not nor cannot use such vigilance
As when they are fresh.

SEBASTIAN. [*Aside to* ANTONIO.] I say tonight. No more.

[*Solemn and strange music. Enter* PROSPERO *on the top,° invisible.*]

ALONSO. What harmony is this? My good friends, hark.

GONZALO. Marvellous sweet music.

[*Enter spirits, in several strange shapes, bringing in a table and a banquet, and dance about it with gentle actions of salutations, and, inviting the King and his companions to eat, they depart.*]

20 **ALONSO.** Give us kind keepers,° heavens! What were these?

SEBASTIAN. A living drollery.° Now I will believe
That there are unicorns; that in Arabia
There is one tree, the phoenix' throne, one phoenix°
At this hour reigning there.

ANTONIO. I'll believe both;
25 And what does else want credit° come to me,
And I'll be sworn 'tis true. Travellers° ne'er did lie,
Though fools at home condemn 'em.

GONZALO. If in Naples
I should report this now, would they believe me—
If I should say I saw such islanders?
30 For certes° these are people of the island,
Who though they are of monstrous shape, yet note
Their manners are more gentle-kind than of

---

13 **advantage** opportunity
14 **throughly** thoroughly
17 **top** a small platform above the stage
20 **keepers** guardian angels
21 **drollery** puppet show or comic picture
23 **phoenix** a mythological Arabian bird of which only one at a time can exist
25 **what does else want credit** whatever else is incredible
26 **Travellers** proverbially reputed to be liars
30 **certes** certainly

Our human generation you shall find
Many, nay, almost any.

PROSPERO. [*Aside.*] Honest lord,
35 Thou hast said well, for some of you there present
Are worse than devils.

ALONSO. I cannot too much muse.°
Such shapes, such gesture, and such sound, expressing—
Although they want the use of tongue—a kind
Of excellent dumb discourse.

PROSPERO. [*Aside.*] Praise in departing.°

40 **FRANCISCO.** They vanished strangely.

SEBASTIAN. No matter, since
They have left their viands° behind, for we have stomachs.°
Will't please you taste of what is here?

ALONSO. Not I.

GONZALO. Faith, sir, you need not fear. When we were boys,
Who would believe that there were mountaineers
45 Dewlapped like bulls, whose throats had hanging at 'em
Wallets° of flesh? Or that there were such men
Whose heads stood in their breasts? Which now we find
Each putter-out of five for one° will bring us
Good warrant of.

ALONSO. [*Rising.*] I will stand to and feed.
50 Although my last—no matter, since I feel
The best is past. Brother, my lord the Duke,
Stand to, and do as we.

[ALONSO, SEBASTIAN, *and* ANTONIO *approach the table. Thunder and lightning. Enter* ARIEL *descending like a harpy,° claps his wings upon the table, and, with a quaint device, the banquet vanishes.*]

---

36 **muse** marvel

39 **Praise in departing** Hold off your praise until the end

41 **viands** food;
stomachs appetites

46 **wallets** loose folds

48 Elizabethan travelers could deposit money with a London broker and be repaid fivefold if they could prove that they reached their destination.

52 **harpy** a mythological monster that is part woman and part bird

ARIEL. You are three men of sin, whom destiny—
That hath to instrument this lower world
55 And what is in't—the never-surfeited sea
Hath caused to belch up you, and on this island
Where man doth not inhabit, you 'mongst men
Being most unfit to live. I have made you mad,
And even with suchlike valour° men hang and drown
60 Their proper selves.°

[*ALONSO, SEBASTIAN, and ANTONIO draw.*]

You fools! I and my fellows
Are ministers of fate. The elements
Of whom your swords are tempered may as well
Wound the loud winds, or with bemocked-at stabs
Kill the still-closing waters, as diminish
65 One dowl° that's in my plume.° My fellow ministers°
Are like invulnerable. If you could hurt,
Your swords are now too massy° for your strengths
And will not be uplifted.

[*ALONSO, SEBASTIAN, and ANTONIO stand amazed.*]

But remember,
For that's my business to you, that you three
70 From Milan did supplant good Prospero;
Exposed unto the sea, which hath requit it,°
Him and his innocent child; for which foul deed,
The powers, delaying not forgetting, have
Incensed the seas and shores, yea, all the creatures,
75 Against your peace. Thee of thy son, Alonso,
They have bereft, and do pronounce by me
Ling'ring perdition°—worse than any death
Can be at once—shall step by step attend
You and your ways; whose wraths to guard you from—
80 Which here in this most desolate isle else falls

---

59 **suchlike valour** the courage of madmen

60 **Their proper selves** themselves

65 **dowl** tiny feather;
plume plumage;
ministers spirits

67 **massy** heavy

71 **requit it** avenged the deed

77 **perdition** starvation

Upon your heads—is nothing but heart's sorrow
And a clear life ensuing.

[*He ascends and vanishes in thunder. Then, to soft music, enter the spirits again, and dance with mocks and mows,*° *and they depart carrying out the table.*]

PROSPERO. Bravely the figure of this harpy hast thou
Performed, my Ariel; a grace it had devouring.°
85 Of my instruction hast thou nothing bated°
In what thou hadst to say. So with good life
And observation strange my meaner ministers
Their several kinds have done. My high charms work,
And these mine enemies are all knit up
90 In their distractions. They now are in my power;
And in these fits I leave them, while I visit
Young Ferdinand, whom they suppose is drowned,
And his and mine loved darling.

[*Exit.* GONZALO, ADRIAN, *and* FRANCISCO *go towards the others.*]

GONZALO. I'th' name of something holy, sir, why stand you
95 In this strange stare?

ALONSO. O, it is monstrous, monstrous!
Methought the billows spoke and told me of it,
The winds did sing it to me, and the thunder,
That deep and dreadful organ-pipe, pronounced
The name of Prosper. It did bass my trespass.°
100 Therefor° my son i'th' ooze is bedded, and
I'll seek him deeper than e'er plummet sounded,
And with him there lie mudded.

[*Exit.*]

SEBASTIAN. But one fiend at a time,
I'll fight their legions o'er.°

ANTONIO. I'll be thy second.

[*Exeunt* SEBASTIAN *and* ANTONIO.]

---

83 **mows** grimaces
84 **grace . . . devouring** By clapping his wings, Ariel created the illusion of devouring the banquet.
85 **bated** omitted
99 **bass my trespass** sing my crime in a low voice
100 **Therefor** for that
103 **o'er** to the end

GONZALO. All three of them are desperate. Their great guilt,
105 Like poison given to work a great time after,
Now 'gins to bite the spirits. I do beseech you
That are of suppler joints, follow them swiftly,
And hinder them from what this ecstasy°
May now provoke them to.

110 **ADRIAN.** Follow, I pray you.

[*Exeunt.*]

---

108 ecstasy madness

Act 4

Scene 1

[*Enter* PROSPERO, FERDINAND, *and* MIRANDA.]

PROSPERO. [*To* FERDINAND.] If I have too austerely° punished you,
Your compensation makes amends, for I
Have given you here a third of mine own life—
Or that for which I live—who° once again
5 I tender° to thy hand. All thy vexations
Were but my trials of thy love, and thou
Hast strangely° stood the test. Here, afore heaven,
I ratify this my rich gift. O Ferdinand,
Do not smile at me that I boast of her,
10 For thou shalt find she will outstrip all praise,
And make it halt° behind her.

FERDINAND. I do believe it
Against an oracle.°

PROSPERO. Then, as my gift and thine own acquisition
Worthily purchased,° take my daughter. But
15 If thou dost break her virgin-knot° before
All sanctimonious ceremonies may
With full and holy rite be ministered,

---

1 **austerely** severely
4 **who** whom
5 **tender** offer
7 **strangely** wonderfully
11 **halt** limp
12 **Against an oracle** even if a prophecy declared otherwise
14 **purchased** earned
15 **virgin-knot** virginity

No sweet aspersion° shall the heavens let fall
To make this contract grow; but barren hate,
20 Sour-eyed disdain, and discord, shall bestrew
The union of your bed with weeds so loathly
That you shall hate it both. Therefore take heed,
As Hymen's° lamps shall light you.

FERDINAND. As I hope
For quiet days, fair issue,° and long life
25 With such love as 'tis now, the murkiest den,
The most opportune place, the strong'st suggestion°
Our worser genius can,° shall never melt
Mine honour into lust to take away
The edge of that day's celebration;
30 When I shall think or° Phoebus' steeds are foundered°
Or night kept chained below.

PROSPERO. Fairly spoke.
Sit, then, and talk with her. She is thine own.

[*FERDINAND and MIRANDA sit and talk together.*]

What,° Ariel, my industrious servant Ariel!

[*Enter ARIEL.*]

ARIEL. What would my potent master? Here I am.

35 **PROSPERO.** Thou and thy meaner fellows° your last service
Did worthily perform, and I must use you
In such another trick. Go bring the rabble,
O'er whom I give thee power, here to this place.
Incite them to quick motion, for I must
40 Bestow upon the eyes of this young couple
Some vanity of mine art.° It is my promise,

---

18 **aspersion** shower (grace)

23 **Hymen's** belonging to the Greek god of marriage

24 **issue** children

26 **suggestion** temptation

27 **worser genius can** bad angel is capable of

30 **or** either;
Phoebus' steeds . . . foundered the horses that pull the chariot of Phoebus, the sun god (On his wedding day, Ferdinand will be impatient for night to come.)

33 **What** now then

35 **meaner fellows** lesser spirits

41 **vanity of mine art** display of magic

And they expect it from me.

ARIEL. Presently°

PROSPERO. Ay, with a twink.°

ARIEL. Before you can say 'Come' and 'Go',
45 And breathe twice, and cry 'So, so',
Each one tripping on his toe
Will be here with mop and mow.°
Do you love me, master? No?

PROSPERO. Dearly, my delicate Ariel. Do not approach
50 Till thou dost hear me call.

ARIEL. Well; I conceive°

[*Exit.*]

PROSPERO. [*To* FERDINAND.] Look thou be true. Do not give dalliance
Too much the rein. The strongest oaths are straw
To th' fire i'th' blood. Be more abstemious,
Or else, good night your vow.

FERDINAND. I warrant you, sir,
55 The white cold virgin snow upon my heart
Abates the ardour of my liver.

PROSPERO. Well.—
Now come, my Ariel! Bring a corollary°
Rather than want a spirit. Appear, and pertly.

[*Soft music.*]

[*To* FERDINAND *and* MIRANDA.] No tongue, all eyes! Be silent.

[*Enter* IRIS.]

60 **IRIS.**° Ceres,° most bounteous lady, thy rich leas°
Of wheat, rye, barley, vetches, oats, and peas;
Thy turfy mountains where live nibbling sheep,

---

42 **Presently** immediately

43 **with a twink** in the twinkling of an eye

47 **mop and mow** grimaces

50 **conceive** understand

57 **corollary** surplus

60 **Iris** Greek goddess of the rainbow and messenger of the gods;
Ceres Roman goddess of agriculture;
leas tracts of land

And flat meads° thatched with stover,° them to keep;
Thy banks with peonied and twillèd brims
65 Which spongy April at thy hest betrims°
To make cold° nymphs chaste crowns; and thy broom-groves,°
Whose shadow the dismissèd bachelor loves,
Being lass-lorn; thy pole-clipped° vineyard.
And thy sea-marge,° sterile and rocky-hard,
70 Where thou thyself dost air:° the Queen o'th' Sky,°
Whose wat'ry arch° and messenger am I,
Bids thee leave these, and with her sovereign grace

[*JUNO appears in the air.*]

Here on this grass-plot, in this very place,
To come and sport.—Her peacocks fly amain.°
75 Approach, rich Ceres, her to entertain.

[*Enter ARIEL as CERES.*]

CERES. Hail, many-coloured messenger, that ne'er
Dost disobey the wife of Jupiter;
Who with thy saffron wings upon my flowers
Diffusest honey-drops, refreshing showers,
80 And with each end of thy blue bow dost crown
My bosky° acres and my unshrubbed down,
Rich scarf to my proud earth. Why hath thy queen
Summoned me hither to this short-grassed green?

IRIS. A contract of true love to celebrate,
85 And some donation freely to estate°
On the blest lovers.

---

63 **meads** meadows;
stover hay

65 **Which . . . betrims** which damp April adorns at your command

66 **cold** chaste;
broom-groves groups of shrubs

68 **pole-clipped** pruned

69 **sea-marge** seashore

70 **air** take the air;
Queen o'th' Sky Juno, Roman goddess of marriage

71 **wat'ry arch** rainbow

74 **amain** in haste (Peacocks were sacred to Juno.)

81 **bosky** covered with bushes

85 **estate** bestow

CERES. Tell me, heavenly bow,°
If Venus or her son,° as thou dost know,
Do not attend the Queen. Since they did plot
The means that dusky Dis° my daughter got,
90 Her and her blind boy's scandalled company
I have forsworn.

IRIS. Of her society
Be not afraid. I met her deity
Cutting the clouds towards Paphos, and her son
Dove-drawn with her. Here thought they to have done
95 Some wanton charm° upon this man and maid,
Whose vows are that no bed-right shall be paid
Till Hymen's torch be lighted°—but in vain.
Mars's hot minion° is returned again.
Her waspish-headed° son has broke his arrows,
100 Swears he will shoot no more, but play with sparrows,
And be a boy right out.

[*Music. JUNO descends to the stage.*]

CERES. Hightest queen of state,
Great Juno, comes; I know her by her gait.

JUNO. How does my bounteous sister? Go with me
To bless this twain, that they may prosperous be,
105 And honoured in their issue.

[*CERES joins JUNO, and they sing.*]

JUNO. Honour, riches, marriage-blessing,
Long continuance and increasing,
Hourly joys be still upon you.
Juno sings her blessings on you.

110 **CERES.** Earth's increase, and foison° plenty,
Barns and garners° never empty

---

86 **bow** rainbow
87 **son** Cupid
89 **Dis** Pluto, god of the underworld, who abducted Ceres' daughter Persephone
94–95 **done . . . charm** cast a lewd spell
97 **Till . . . lighted** until the wedding ceremony is performed
98 **Mars's hot minion** Venus
99 **waspish-headed** peevish
110 **foison** abundance
111 **garners** grain bins

Vines with clust'ring bunches growing,
Plants with goodly burden bowing;
Spring come to you at the farthest,
115 In the very end of harvest
Scarcity and want shall shun you,
Ceres' blessing so is on you.

FERDINAND. This is a most majestic vision, and
Harmounious charmingly. May I be bold
120 To think these spirits?

PROSPERO. Spirits, which by mine art
I have from their confines called to enact
My present fancies.

FERDINAND. Let me live here ever!
So rare a wondered father and a wise
Makes this place paradise.

[*JUNO and CERES whisper, and send IRIS on employment.*]

PROSPERO. Sweet now, silence.
125 Juno and Ceres whisper seriously.
There's something else to do. Hush, and be mute,
Or else our spell is marred.

IRIS. You nymphs called naiads° of the wind'ring brooks,
With your sedged crowns and ever-harmless looks,
130 Leave your crisp channels, and on this green land
Answer your summons; Juno does command.
Come, temperate nymphs, and help to celebrate
A contract of true love. Be not too late.

[*Enter certain nymphs.*]

You sunburned sicklemen,° of August weary,
135 Come hither from the furrow and be merry;
Make holiday, your rye-straw hats put on,
And these fresh nymphs encounter every one
In country footing.°

[*Enter certain reapers, properly habited.° They join with the nymphs in a graceful dance; towards the end whereof PROSPERO starts suddenly, and speaks.*]

---

128 **naiads** water nymphs
134 **sicklemen** harvesters
138 **footing** dancing
139 **habited** dressed

PROSPERO. [*Aside.*] I had forgot that foul conspiracy
140 Of the beast Caliban and his confederates
Against my life. The minute of their plot
Is almost come. [*To the spirits.*] Well done! Avoid; no more!

[*To a strange, hollow, and confused noise, the spirits in the pageant heavily vanish.* FERDINAND *and* MIRANDA *rise.*]

FERDINAND. [*To* MIRANDA.] This is strange. Your father's in some passion
That works him strongly.

MIRANDA. Never till this day
145 Saw I him touched with anger so distempered.

PROSPERO. You do look, my son, in a moved sort,°
As if you were dismayed. Be cheerful, sir.
Our revels° now are ended. These our actors,
As I foretold you, were all spirits, and
150 Are melted into air, into thin air;
And like the baseless fabric of this vision,
The cloud-capped towers, the gorgeous palaces,
The solemn temples, and the great globe itself,
Yea, all which it inherit, shall dissolve;
155 And, like this insubstantial pageant faded,
Leave not a rack° behind. We are such stuff
As dreams are made on,° and our little life
Is rounded with a sleep. Sir, I am vexed.
Bear with my weakness. My old brain is troubled.
160 Be not disturbed with my infirmity.
If you be pleased, retire into my cell,
And there repose. A turn or two I'll walk
To still my beating mind.

FERDINAND and **MIRANDA.** We wish your peace.

[*Exeunt* FERDINAND *and* MIRANDA.]

PROSPERO. Come with a thought!° I thank thee, Ariel. Come!

[*Enter* ARIEL.]

---

146 **moved sort** troubled state
148 **revels** entertainment
156 **rack** cloud
157 **on** of
164 **with a thought** in an instant

165 **ARIEL.** Thy thoughts I cleave to. What's thy pleasure?

PROSPERO. Spirit,
We must prepare to meet with Caliban.

ARIEL. Ay, my commander. When I presented Ceres
I thought to have told thee of it, but I feared
Lest I might anger thee.

170 **PROSPERO.** Say again: where didst thou leave these varlets?°

ARIEL. I told you, sir, they were red-hot with drinking;
So full of valour that they smote° the air
For breathing in their faces, beat the ground
For kissing of their feet; yet always bending°
175 Towards their project. Then I beat my tabor,
At which like unbacked° colts they pricked their ears,
Advanced° their eyelids,lifted up their noses
As they smelt music. So I chared their ears
That calf-like they my lowing° followed, through
180 Toothed briars, sharp furzes, pricking gorse,° and thorns,
Which entered their frail shins. At last I left them
I'th' filty-mantled pool beyond your cell,
There dancing up to th' chins, that the foul lake
O'er-stunk° their feet.

PROSPERO. This was well done, my bird.
185 Thy shape invisible retain thou still.
The trumpery° in my house, go bring it hither
For stale° to catch these thieves.

ARIEL. I go, I go.

PROSPERO. A devil, a born devil, on whose nature
Nurture can never stick; on whom my pains,

---

170 **varlets** rascals
172 **smote** struck
174 **bending** aiming
176 **unbacked** unbroken
177 **Advanced** raised
179 **lowing** mooing
180 **Toothed briars . . . gorse** types of prickly shrubs
184 **O'er-stunk** stunk worse than
186 **trumpery** worthless finery
187 **stale** decoy

190 Humanely taken, all, all lost, quite lost,
And, as with age his body uglier grows,
So his mind cankers. I will plague them all,
Even to roaring.

[*Enter* ARIEL, *laden with glistening apparel, etc.*]

Come, hang them on this lime.°

[ARIEL *hangs up the apparel. Exeunt* PROSPERO *and* ARIEL. *Enter* CALIBAN, STEFANO, *and* TRINCULO, *all wet.*]

CALIBAN. Pray you, tread softly, that the blind mole may
195 Not hear a foot fall. We now are near his cell.

STEFANO. Monster, your fairy, which you say is a harmless fairy, has done little better than played the Jack with us.°

TRINCULO. Monster, I do smell all horse-piss, at which my nose is in a great indignation.

200 **STEFANO.** So is mine. Do you hear, monster? If I should take a displeasure against you, look you—

TRINCULO. Thou wert but a lost monster.

CALIBAN. Good my lord, give me thy favour still.
Be patient, for the prize I'll bring thee to
205 Shall hoodwink° this mischance. Therefore speak softly.
All's hushed as midnight yet.

TRINCULO. Ay, but to lose our bottles in the pool!

STEFANO. There is not only disgrace and dishounour in that, monster, but an infinite loss.

210 **TRINCULO.** That's more to me than my wetting. Yet this is your harmless fairy, monster.

STEFANO. I will fetch off° my bottle, though I be o'er ears° for my labour.

CALIBAN. Prithee, my king, be quiet. Seest thou here;
215 This is the mouth o'th' cell. No noise, and enter.
Do that good mischief which may make this island

---

193 **lime** lime tree

197 **played the Jack with us** made fools of us

205 **hoodwink** put out of sight and mind

212 **fetch off** recover;
o'er ears drowned

Thine own for ever, and I thy Caliban
For aye thy foot-licker.

STEFANO. Give me thy hand.
I do begin to have bloody thoughts.

220 **TRINCULO.** [*Seeing the apparel.*] O King Stefano, O peer! O worthy Stefano, look what a wardrobe here is for thee!

CALIBAN. Let it alone, thou fool, it is but trash.

TRINCULO. [*Putting on a gown.*] O ho, monster, we know what belongs to a frippery!° O King Stefano!

225 **STEFANO.** Put off that gown, Trinculo. By this hand, I'll have that gown.

TRINCULO. Thy grace shall have it.

CALIBAN. The dropsy° drown this fool! What do you mean
To dote this on such luggage?° Let't alone,
230 And do the murder first. If he awake,
From toe to crown he'll fill our skins with pinches,
Make us strange stuff.

STEFANO. Be you quiet, monster,—Mistress lime, is not this my jerkin?° Now is the jerkin under the line. Now, jerkin, you are
235 like to lose your hair and prove a bald jerkin.

[*STEFANO and TRINCULO take garments.*]

TRINCULO. Do, do! We steal by line and level, an't like your grace.

STEFANO. I thank thee for that jest. Here's a garment for't. Wit shall not go unrewarded while I am king of this country. 'Steal
240 by line and level' is an excellent pass of pate.° There's another garment for't.

TRINCULO. Monster, come, put some lime upon your fingers,° and away with the rest.

CALIBAN. I will have none on't. We shall lose our time,
245 And all be turned to barnacles, or to apes
With foreheads villainous low.

---

224 **frippery** shop selling used clothing (He doesn't agree that the clothes are trash.)
227 **dropsy** a disease that causes excess fluid to accumulate in tissues
229 **luggage** encumbrance
234 **jerkin** close-fitting jacket
240 **pass of pate** clever thrust
241 **put . . . fingers** be sticky-fingered

STEFANO. Monster, lay to° your fingers. Help to bear this away where my hogshead of wine is, or I'll turn you out of my kingdom. Go to, carry this.

250 **TRINCULO.** And this.

STEFANO. Ay, and this.

[*They load* CALIBAN *with apparel. A noise of hunters heard. Enter divers° spirits in shape of dogs and hounds, hunting them about;* PROSPERO *and* ARIEL *setting them on.*]

PROSPERO. Hey, Mountain, hey!

ARIEL. Silver! There it goes, Silver!

PROSPERO. Fury, Fury! There, Tyrant, there! Hark, hark!

[*Exeunt* STEFANO, TRINCULO, *and* CALIBAN, *pursued by spirits.*]

[*To* ARIEL.] Go, charge my goblins that they grind their joints
255 With dry convulsions, shorten up their sinews
With agèd cramps, and more pinch-spotted° make them
Than pard or cat o'mountain.°

[*Cries within.*]

ARIEL. Hark, they roar!

PROSPERO. Let them be hunted soundly. At this hour
Lies at my mercy all mine enemies.
260 Shortly shall all my labours end, and thou
Shalt have the air at freedom. For a little,
Follow, and do me service.

[*Exeunt.*]

---

247 **lay to** apply

251 **divers** various

256 **pinch-spotted** bruised by pinches

257 **pard or cat o'mountain** both are terms for the leopard

Act 5

Scene 1

[*Enter* PROSPERO, *in his magic robes, and* ARIEL.]

PROSPERO. Now does my project gather to a head.
My charms crack not, my spirits obey, and time
Goes upright with his carriage.° How's the day?

ARIEL. On the sixth hour; at which time, my lord,
5 You said our work should cease.

PROSPERO. I did say so
When first I raised the tempest. Say, my spirit,
How fares the King and's followers?

ARIEL. Confined together
In the same fashion as you gave in charge,
Just as you left them; all prisoners, sir,
10 In the lime-grove which weather-fends° your cell.
They cannot budge till your release.° The King,
His brother, and yours, abide all three distracted,°
And the remainder mourning over them
Brimful of sorrow and dismay; but chiefly
15 Him that you termed, sir, the good old lord Gonzalo:
His tears run down his beard like winter's drops
From eaves of reeds.° Your charm so strongly works 'em
That if you now beheld them your affections
Would become tender.

PROSPERO. Dost thou think so, spirit?

---

3 **Goes . . . carriage** walks without stooping (because his burden is light)
10 **weather-fends** protects from the weather
11 **your release** you release them
12 **distracted** deranged
17 **eaves of reeds** thatched roofs

20 **ARIEL.** Mine would, sir, were I human.

PROSPERO. And mine shall.
Hast thou, which art but air, a touch, a feeling
Of their afflictions, and shall not myself,
One of their kind, that relish all as sharply
Passion as they,° be kindlier moved than thou art?
25 Though with their high wrongs I am struck to th' quick,
Yet with my nobler reason 'gainst my fury
Do I take part. The rarer action is
In virtue than in vengeance. They being penitent,
The sole drift of my purpose doth extend
30 Not a frown further. Go release them, Ariel.
My charms I'll break, their senses I'll restore,
And they shall be themselves.

ARIEL. I'll fetch them, sir.

[*Exit.* PROSPERO *draws a circle with his staff.*]

PROSPERO. Ye elves of hills, brooks, standing lakes and groves,
And ye that on the sands with printless foot
35 Do chase the ebbing Neptune,° and do fly° him
When he comes back; you demi-puppets that
By moonshine do the green sour ringlets° make
Whereof the ewe not bites; and you whose pastime
Is to make midnight mushrooms,° that° rejoice
40 To hear the solemn curfew,° by whose aid,
Weak masters though ye be, I have bedimmed
The noontide sun, called forth the mutinous winds,
And 'twixt the green sea and the azured vault°
Set roaring war—to the dread rattling thunder
45 Have I given fire, and rifted° Jove's stout oak
With his own bolt, the strong-based promontory

23–24 **that relish . . . they** who feel suffering as keenly as they do

35 **ebbing Neptune** retreating tide;
fly flee from

37 **green sour ringlets** circles of sour grass called "fairy rings."

39 **midnight mushrooms** mushrooms that appear overnight;
that you who

40 **solemn curfew** the evening bell (which marks the hour when spirits are free to roam)

43 **azured vault** blue sky

45 **rifted** split

Have I made shake, and by the spurs° plucked up
The pine and cedar; graves at my command
Have waked their sleepers, oped, and let 'em forth
50 By my so potent art. But this rough magic
I here abjure. And when I have required
Some heavenly music—which even now I do—
To work mine end upon their senses that
This airy charm is for,° I'll break my staff,
55 Bury it certain fathoms in the earth,
And deeper than did ever plummet sound
I'll drown my book.

[*Solemn music. Here enters first* ARIEL *invisible; then* ALONSO, *with a frantic gesture, attended by* GONZALO; SEBASTIAN *and* ANTONIO, *in the manner, attended by* ADRIAN *and* FRANCISCO. *They all enter the circle which* PROSPERO *had made, and there stand charmed; which* PROSPERO *observing, speaks*.]

[*To* ALONSO.] A solemn air, and the best comforter
To an unsettled fancy, cure thy brains,
60 Now useless, boiled within thy skull.
[*To* SEBASTIAN *and* ANTONIO.] There stand,
For you are spell-stopped.—
Holy Gonzalo, honourable man,
Mine eyes, ev'n sociable to the show of thine,
Fall fellowly drops.° [*Aside*.] The charm dissolves apace,
65 And as the morning steals upon the night,
Melting the darkness, so their rising senses
Begin to chase the ignorant fumes° that mantle°
Their clearer reason.—O good Gonzalo,
My true preserver, and a loyal sir
70 To him thou follow'st, I will pay thy graces
Home° both in word and deed.—Most cruelly
Didst thou, Alonso, use me and my daughter,
Thy brother was a further in the act.—
Thou art pinched for't now, Sebastian.
[*To* ANTONIO.] Flesh and blood,

---

47 **spurs** roots

53–54 **their senses . . . for** the senses of those whom this music is for

63–64 **Mine eyes . . . drops** I cry because you cry.

67 **ignorant fumes** fogs of ignorance;
mantle cover

70–71 **pay . . . Home** fully repay your favors

75 You, brother mine, that entertained ambition,
Expelled remorse and nature, whom, with Sebastian—
Whose inward pinches° therefore are most strong,—
Would here have killed your king, I do forgive thee,
Unnatural though thou art. [*Aside.*] Their understanding
80 Begins to swell, and the approaching tide
Will shortly fill the reasonable shores
That now lie foul and muddy. Not one of them
That yet looks on me, or would know me.—Ariel,
Fetch me the hat and rapier in my cell.
85 I will discase me,° and myself present
As I was sometime Milan.° Quickly, spirit!
Thou shalt ere long be free.

[*Ariel sings and helps to attire him as Duke of Milan.*]

ARIEL. Where the bee sucks, there suck I:
In a cowslip's bell I lie;
90 There I couch when owls do cry.
On the bat's back I do fly
After summer merrily.
Merrily, merrily shall I live now
Under the blossom that hangs on the bough.
95 Merrily, merrily shall I live now
Under the blossom that hangs on the bough.

PROSPERO. Why, that's my dainty Ariel! I shall miss thee,
But yet thou shalt have freedom.—So, so, so.—
To the King's ship, invisible as thou art!
100 There shalt thou find the mariners asleep
Under the hatches. The Master and the Boatswain
Being awake, enforce them to this place,
And presently, I prithee.

ARIEL. I drink the air before me, and return
105 Or ere your pulse twice beat.

[*Exit.*]

GONZALO. All torment, trouble, wonder, and amazement
Inhabits here. Some heavenly power guide us
Out of this fearful country!

---

77 **inward pinches** guilt

85 **discase me** remove my magic robes

86 **sometime Milan** formerly when Duke of Milan

PROSPERO. Behold, sir King,
The wrongèd Duke of Milan, Prospero.
110 For more assurance that a living prince
Does not speak to thee, I embrace thy body;
And to thee and thy company I bid
A hearty welcome.

[*He embraces* ALONSO.]

ALONSO. Whe'er thou beest he or no,
Or some enchanted trifle° to abuse° me,
115 As late I have been, I not know. Thy pulse
Beats as of flesh and blood; and since I saw thee
Th'affliction of my mind amends, with which
I fear a madness held me. This must crave—
An if this be at all—a most strange story.°
120 Thy dukedom° I resign, and do entreat
Thou pardon me my wrongs. But how should Prospero
Be living and be here?

PROSPERO. [*To* GONZALO.] First, noble friend,
Let me embrace thine age,° whose honour cannot
Be measured or confined.

[*He embraces* GONZALO.]

GONZALO. Whether this be
125 Or be not, I'll not swear.

PROSPERO. You do yet taste
Some subtleties° o'th' isle that will not let you
Believe things certain.—Welcome, my friends all.

[*Aside to* SEBASTIAN *and* ANTONIO.]

But you, my brace° of lords, were I so minded,
I here could pluck his highness' frown upon you
130 And justify° you traitors. At this time
I will tell no tales.

---

114 **trifle** illusion
abuse deceive

118–119 **This must . . . story** If this is real, then it requires a strange explanation

120 **Thy dukedom** my right to tribute from your dukedom

123 **age** seniority

126 **subtleties** deceptions

128 **brace** pair

130 **justify** prove

SEBASTIAN [*To* ANTONIO.] The devil speaks in him.

PROSPERO. No.
[*To* ANTONIO.] For you, most wicked sir, whom to call brother
Would even infect my mouth, I do forgive
Thy rankest fault, all of them, and require
135 My dukedom of thee, which perforce° I know
Thou must restore.

ALONSO. If thou beest Prospero,
Give us particulars of thy preservation,
How thou hast met us here, whom three hours since
Were wrecked upon this shore, where I have lost—
140 How sharp the point of this remembrance is!—
My dear son Ferdinand.

PROSPERO. I am woe for't sir.

ALONSO. Irreparable is the loss, and patience
Says it is past her cure.

PROSPERO. I rather think
You have not sought her help, of whose soft grace
145 For the like loss I have her sovereign aid,
And rest myself content.

ALONSO. You the like loss?

PROSPERO. As great to me as late; and supportable
To make the dear loss have I means much weaker°
Than you may call to comfort you, for I
150 Have lost my daughter.

ALONSO. A daughter?
O heavens, that they were living both in Naples,
The kind and queen there! That they were, I wish
Myself were mudded in that oozy bed
Where my son lies. When did you lose your daughter?

155 **PROSPERO.** In this last tempest. I perceive these lords
At this encounter do so much admire°
That they devour their reason and scarce think
Their eyes do offices of truth, these words
Are natural breath. But howsoe'er you have

---

135 **perforce** of necessity

147–148 **supportable . . . weaker** I have much weaker means to make the grievous loss bearable

156 **admire** wonder

160 Been jostled from your senses, know for certain
That I am Prospero, and that very Duke
Which was thrust forth of Milan, who most strangely,
Upon this shore where you were wrecked, was landed
To be the lord on't. No more yet of this,
165 For 'tis a chronicle of day by day,
Not a relation° for a breakfast, nor
Befitting this first meeting. Welcome, sir.
This cell's my court. Here have I few attendants,
And subjects none abroad.° Pray you, look in.
170 My dukedom since you have given me again.
I will requite you with as good a thing;
At least bring forth a wonder to content ye
As much as me my dukedom.

[*Here* PROSPERO *discovers*° FERDINAND *and* MIRANDA, *playing at chess*.]

MIRANDA. Sweet lord, you play me false.

175 **FERDINAND.** No, my dearest love,
I would not for the world.

MIRANDA. Yes, for a score of kingdoms you should wrangle,
An I would call it fair play.

ALONSO. If this prove
A vision of the island, one dear son
180 Shall I twice lose.

SEBASTIAN. A most high miracle.

FERDINAND. [*Coming forward.*] Though the seas threaten, they are merciful.
I have cursed them without cause.

[*He kneels.*]

ALONSO. Now all the blessings
Of a glad father compass° thee about.
Arise and say how thou cam'st here.

[FERDINAND *rises.*]

MIRANDA. [*Coming forward.*] O wonder!

---

166 **relation** tale
169 **abroad** elsewhere
174 **discovers** reveals by drawing back a curtain
183 **compass** surround

185 How many goodly creatures are there here!
How beauteous mankind is! O brave new world
That has such people in't!

PROSPERO. 'Tis new to thee.

ALONSO. [*To* FERDINAND.] What is this maid with whom thou wast at play?
Your eld'st acquaintance cannot be three hours.
190 Is she the goddess that hath severed us,
And brought us thus together?

FERDINAND. Sir, she is mortal;
But by immortal providence she's mine.
I chose her when I could not ask my father
For his advice, nor thought I had one. She
195 Is daughter to his famous Duke of Milan,
Of who so often I have heard renown,
But never saw before; of whom I have
Received a second life; and second father
This lady makes him to me.

ALONSO. I am hers.°
200 But O, how oddly will it sound, that I
Must ask my child forgiveness!

PROSPERO. There, sir, stop.
Let us not burden our remembrance with
A heaviness that's gone.

GONZALO. I have inly wept,
Or should have spoke ere this. Look down, you gods,
205 And on this couple drop a blessèd crown,
For it is you that have chalked forth the way
Which brought us hither.

ALONSO. I say amen, Gonzalo.

GONZALO. Was Milan° thrust from Milan, that his issue°
Should become kings of Naples? O rejoice
210 Beyond a common joy! And set it down
With gold on lasting pillars; in one voyage
Did Claribel her husband find at Tunis,
And Ferdinand her brother found a wife

---

199 **I am hers** I am her second father.

208 **Milan** the Duke of Milan;
issue descendants

Where he himself was lost; Prospero his dukedom
215 In a poor isle; and all of us ourselves,
When no man was his own.°

ALONSO. [*To* FERDINAND *and* MIRANDA.] Give me your hands.
Let grief and sorrow still embrace his heart
That doth not wish you joy.

GONZALO. Be it so! Amen!

[*Enter* ARIEL, *with the* MASTER *and* BOATSWAIN *amazedly following.*]

O look, sir, look, sir, here is more of us!
220 I prophesied if a gallows were on land
This fellow could not drown. [*To the* BOASTSWAIN.] Now, blasphemy,
That swear'st grace o'erboard: not an oath on shore?
Hast thou no mouth by land? What is the news?

BOATSWAIN. The best news is that we have safely found
225 Our King and company. The next, our ship,
Which but three glasses since we gave out split,°
Is tight and yare° and bravely rigged, as when
We first put out to sea.

ARIEL. [*Aside to* PROSPERO.] Sir, all this service
Have I done since I went.

PROSPERO. [*Aside to* ARIEL.] My tricksy spirit!

230 **ALONSO.** These are not natural events; they strengthen
From strange to stranger. Say, how came you hither?

BOATSWAIN. If I did think, sir, I were well awake
I'd strive to tell you. We were dead of sleep,
And—how we know not—all clapped° under hatches,
235 Where but even now, with strange and several noises
Of roaring, shrieking, howling, jingling chains,
And more diversity of sounds, all horrible,
We were awaked; straightway at liberty;
Where we in all trim° freshly beheld
240 Our royal, good, and gallant ship, our Master

---

216 **When . . . own** when we had lost our senses
226 **Which . . . split** which only three hours ago we declared split
227 **tight and yare** watertight and seaworthy
234 **clapped** shut away
239 **trim** undamaged condition

Cap'ring to eye her.° On a trice,° so please you,
Even in a dream, were we devided from them,
And were brought moping° hither.

ARIEL. [*Aside to* PROSPERO.] Was't well done?

PROSPERO. [*Aside to* ARIEL.] Bravely, my diligence. Thou shalt be free.

245 **ALONSO.** This is as strange a maze as e'er men trod,
And there is in this business more than nature
Was ever conduct of. Some oracle
Must rectify our knowledge.

PROSPERO. Sir, my liege,
Do not infest your mind with beating on
250 The strangeness of this business. At picked leisure,
Which shall be shortly, single° I'll resolve you,°
Which to you shall seem probable, of every
These happened accidents,° till when be cheerful,
And think of each thing well. [*Aside to* ARIEL.] Come hither, spirit.
255 Set Caliban and his companions free.
Untie the spell.

[*Exit* ARIEL.]

[*To* ALONSO.] How fares my gracious sir?
There are yet missing of your company
Some few odd lads that you remember not.

[*Enter* ARIEL, *driving in* CALIBAN, STEFANO, *and* TRINCULO, *in their stolen apparel.*]

STEFANO. Every man shift for all the rest, and let no man take
260 care for himself, for all is but fortune. Coragio, bully-monster,°
coragio!

TRINCULO. If these be true spies° which I wear in my head, here's a goodly sight.

---

241 **Cap'ring to eye her** dancing for joy upon seeing her;
On a trice In an instant

243 **moping** dazed

251 **single** privately;
resolve you explain to you

253 **happened accidents** events that have occurred

260 **Coragio, bully-monster** Courage, excellent monster!

262 **true spies** trustworthy observers

CALIBAN. O Setebos,° these be brave spirits indeed!
265 How fine° my master is! I am afraid
He will chastise me.

SEBASTIAN. Ha, ha! What things are these, my lord Antonio?
Will money buy 'em?

ANTONIO. Very like; one of them
Is a plain fish, and no doubt marketable.

270 **PROSPERO.** Mark but the badges° of these men, my lords,
Then say if they be true. This misshapen knave,
His mother was a witch, and one so strong
That could control the moon, make flows and ebbs,
And deal in her command without her power.°
275 These three have robbed me, and this demi-devil,
For he's a bastard one, had plotted with them
To take my life. Two of these fellows you
Must know and own. This thing of darkness I
Acknowledge mine.

CALIBAN. I shall be pinched to death.

280 **ALONSO.** Is not this Stefano, my drunken butler?

SEBASTIAN. He is drunk now. Where had he wine?

ALONSO. And Trinculo is reeling ripe.° Where should they
Find this grand liquor that hath gilded 'em?°
[*To* TRINCULO.] How cam'st thou in this pickle?

285 **TRINCULO.** I have been in such a pickle since I saw you last that,
I fear me, will never out of my bones. I shall not fear fly-
blowing.°

SEBASTIAN. Why, how now, Stefano?

STEFANO. O, touch me not! I am not Stefano, but a cramp.

290 **PROSPERO.** You'd be king o'the isle, sirrah?

---

264 **Setebos** Caliban's god
265 **fine** splendidly dressed
270 **badges** identifying emblems worn by servants of noblemen
274 **deal . . . power** exercise the moon's authority outside of her control
282 **reeling ripe** drunk enough to be reeling
283 **gilded them** made them red-faced
287 **fly-blowing** being infested by flies like rotten meat

STEFANO. I should have been a sore one, then.

ALONSO. [*Pointing to* CALIBAN.] This is a strange thing as e'er I looked on.

PROSPERO. He is as disproportioned in his manners
295 As in his shape. [*To* CALIBAN.] Go, sirrah, to my cell.
Take with you your companions. As you look
To have my pardon, trim° it handsomely.

CALIBAN. Ay, that I will; and I'll be wise hereafter,
And seek for grace. What a thrice-double ass
300 Was I to take this drunkard for a god,
And worship this dull fool!

PROSPERO. Go to, away!

[*Exit* CALIBAN.]

ALONSO. [*To* STEFANO *and* TRINCULO.]
Hence, and bestow your luggage° where you found it.

SEBASTIAN. Or stole it, rather.

[*Exeunt* STEFANO *and* TRUNCULO.]

PROSPERO. [*To* ALONSO.] Sir, I invite your highness and your train
305 To my poor cell, where you shall take your rest
For this one night; which part of it I'll waste°
With such discourse as I not doubt shall make it
Go quick away: the story of my life,
And the particular accidents gone by
310 Since I came to this isle. And in the morn
I'll bring you to your ship, and so to Naples,
Where I have hope to see the nuptial
Of these our dear-belovèd solemnized;°
And thence retire me to my Milan, where
315 Every third thought shall be my grave.

---

297 **trim** prepare

302 **luggage** the stolen clothes

306 **which part . . . waste** part of which I'll occupy

312–313 **the nuptial . . . solemnized** the wedding ceremony of our loved ones

ALONSO. I long
To hear the story of your life, which must
Take the ear strangely.

PROSPERO. I'll deliver all,
And promise you calm seas, auspicious gales,
And sail so expeditious that shall catch
320 Your royal fleet far off. [*Aside to* ARIEL.] My Ariel, chick,
That is thy charge. Then to the elements
Be free, and fare thou well.

[*Exit* ARIEL.]

Please you, draw near.

[*Exeunt all but* PROSPERO.]

Epilogue

PROSPERO. Now my charms are all o'erthrown,
And what strength I have's mine own,
Which is most faint. Now 'tis true
I must be here confined by you
5 Or sent to Naples. Let me not,
Since I have my dukedom got,
And pardoned the deceiver, dwell
In this bare island° by your spell;
But release me from my bands°
10 With the help of your good hands.°
Gentle breath° of yours my sails
Must fill, or else my project fails
Which was to please. Now I want
Spirits to enforce, art to enchant;
15 And my ending is despair
Unless I be relieved by prayer,°
Which pierces so, that it assaults
Mercy itself, and frees all faults.
As you from crimes would pardoned be,
20 Let your indulgence° set me free.

[*He awaits applause, then exit.*]

---

8 **bare island** the stage

9 **bands** bonds

10 **good hands** applause

11 **Gentle breath** kind words

15–16 **my ending . . . prayer** This performance will be a failure unless you respond to my plea for approval.

20 **indulgence** pardon (in the form of applause)

Related Readings

Patrick Pacheco

Two Control Freaks Take on Shakespeare

In this article from Newsday, *actor Patrick Stewart and director George Wolfe discuss the motivations and inspirations behind their 1995 stage production of* The Tempest.

TALK ABOUT BRAVE new worlds. Director George Wolfe and actor Patrick Stewart might well have come from opposite ends of the galaxy, blown together by the production of Shakespeare's *The Tempest* at the Delacorte in Central Park. After all, Stewart, long before he became internationally famous as Captain Jean Luc Picard of the Starship Enterprise, was a Royal Shakespeare Company [RSC] veteran who'd done 26 of Shakespeare's 40 plays. His Broadway debut was in Peter Brook's seminal[1] 1971 production of *A Midsummer Night's Dream*, and this is his fourth *Tempest*, his second as Prospero, the exiled duke who rules over his island prison with magic. Although this is Wolfe's third year at the helm of the New York Shakespeare Festival, the production marks his debut as a director of the Bard's work. Just prior to a recent performance, the director and actor talked about their collaboration on this play, in which Prospero seeks revenge on his evil brother through his magical command of the island's enslaved spirits. The sprite-like Wolfe was a torrent[2] of percolating[3] ideas studded with self-mockery. Stewart, rather majestic in speech and form even in jeans and a T-shirt, was passionate and precise. A wondrously odd couple, indeed.

1. **seminal** creative; contributing to later development
2. **torrent** stream; flow
3. **percolating** bubbling

Stewart: My first encounter with Shakespeare was on the radio, and it was *The Tempest,* with John Gielgud playing Prospero. I must've been eleven or twelve, and there were things that I didn't understand, but I never felt that I was encountering an alien language. I had a brother, sixteen years older, who like me was a working-class boy with little or no education. But he was in the Royal Air Force during the war, and rubbed shoulders with guys who had an interest in music and drama and poetry and art. And so when he came home on leave, he'd read me bedtime stories, and what he read was Shakespeare. So at the age of seven or eight, I was familiar with all of Hamlet's soliloquies.

Wolfe: My father would quote Shakespeare randomly in the course of a conversation, something he'd learned from high school or college. But I remember when I was eleven, I made a point of reading *A Midsummer Night's Dream* one Sunday evening in our home. Frankfort, Kentucky, is not exactly the cultural capital of the world, so my first live encounter was a not-very-good college production of *Othello*. I remember the dichotomy[4] of sitting there, thinking "This is a really ghastly production," at the same time being completely overwhelmed by the language and the stakes and reality. I was on the edge of my seat, even though *Othello* is not one of my favorite plays. I mean, he gives it all up for a handkerchief. Please! Patrick is going to explain it to me so that I will like it better.

Stewart: No, I'm not going to explain it to you. I'm going to make a proposition to you when we have time to talk about it.

Newsday: What's the proposition?

Wolfe: Please! We're not going to tell you. This is a private conversation.

Newsday: Sounds like you might be cooking up another collaboration. Patrick, how did this one differ from your previous experience of playing Prospero?

Stewart: What has happened here, happily, is that original feelings I had about the role when I did it eight or nine years ago have been more realized here because they happen to coincide with strong feelings that George had too. We have taken the emotionality of the man further than I even thought it should go. And I always knew that Prospero was a man who was very much driven by his feelings as much as he was by the brain. Usually, you get a totally cerebral[5] performance.

Wolfe: Prospero sets into motion a whole series of things that are supposed to happen in a certain way, and he ends up being caught because

---

4. **dichotomy** division into two parts

5. **cerebral** intellectual

things get totally thrown off. And when that happens to control freaks, all of the emotions that have driven us to become control freaks all of a sudden erupt and come to the surface. I, of course, have only read about this, not being a control freak myself at all. (Laughs.) But I think it's just so fascinating how much people are controlled by their histories, as Prospero is, and it's something as an American and a person of color, that I am aware of as well.

Stewart: The way I've played Shakespeare up to now was totally informed by the fact that I came from a blue-collar background, felt myself to be a second-class citizen who didn't have a right to certain privileges. My first formal encounters with Shakespeare was through very smart Oxford graduates who were running the RSC at the time, and so, even though I'm really glad to have those influences, I'm now getting more in touch with those original emotional connections rather than the academic ones I learned during my fifteen years with the RSC.

Newsday: How has working with George helped you to do that?

Stewart: Well, directly. Because one of the things I think English training does is that it teaches actors to cheat brilliantly. Through the emphasis on language and text and intellectual understanding, we become very good at pretending. But one of the reasons I'm happy to be staying and working in America and in New York, in particular, is the emotional collisions going on. Tapping into that in this character is not always pleasant. And that's because there are these feelings Prospero has, and they're very uncomfortable and I wake up in the morning and I think, I don't really want to go there. But, for me, as an actor, if I don't at least attempt to go there, I count myself as a fraud.

Wolfe: In our first conversation, Patrick said, "I don't want to play a kindly old gentleman in a beard." And I said, "Well, I'm not interested in directing a kindly old gentleman in a beard." That was, for me, boom, when the journey began. And at one point, Patrick said to me, "I think Prospero is a very angry man." And I felt that way too, of course. You know, I love angry people, being one myself. Here is a man with extraordinarily complicated emotions—rage, revenge, love, hate—a man who every single time he's trusted someone—not to get so Freudian and Oprah on you—there has been a violation and betrayal. So when he comes to this new world, he's an exaggerated version of a control freak. But we catch him at a time, to say the least, when the natives are restless.

Stewart: For me, that's when the most interesting things happen to Prospero, when he is no longer in control, when he says, "Go, release them, Ariel. My charms I'll break, their senses are restored and they shall be themselves." Now that is a terrifying concept! He is preparing to come face to face with people who are what they are, not people in his power.

Newsday: Not that either of you are control freaks, of course, but what happened when you confronted your own desires to play it safe, or "cheat" as you put it.

Wolfe: At the Public, I've turned into Mr. Solution Man. Give me three problems and the brain clicks in and I've become very skilled at doing cosmetic surgery. You put makeup on the problems and the audience goes "bravo," and I was very intent on not doing that, because I want to be not just a smart artist but a good one, and the way I do that is by surrendering my desire to be in complete command. Go on a journey with the help of very smart, very in-touch actors.

Stewart: What I've enjoyed about this relationship with George is that sometimes he will make only a half-reference and I will get it, viscerally,[6] not intellectually. That's one of the ways I've changed as an actor. I will now do anything, try anything.

Wolfe: There were two things I remember very specifically during rehearsals. It was in that first scene where Prospero tells his story, which can be the most tedious[7] scene on the planet, because it's history, history, history. One day, Patrick came to me and said, "I've been thinking about the first time I say, 'my brother.' I think that's an eruption." And I said, "Fine, fine, let's try it." And he's telling the story, and suddenly, there is this California earthquake. "My Brother!" It's a startling and brilliant choice. In that same scene, I suggested to Patrick, "Feel free to move." And he said, "I don't feel the need to move." And I said, "Well, I've got an instinct. Start moving, if you can, and let's see what happens." And Patrick started to move, and what it produced, cut free inside of him, was this emotional churning, which ended up being connected to that brother thing. I opened the door to another way into the scene to take full advantage of that door he'd opened.

Stewart: What you spotted, in fact, was that the stillness of this scene was acting as a barrier to really unlocking the emotions. As long as I was standing still, I was safe. The moment I began to move, I began to lose control of these feelings. They began to control me. I knew the minute I tried it, it felt right.

Newsday: It seemed that it is just this sort of "visceral muscularity" that George has stamped on the Public during his tenure. He's not afraid to go over the top.

---

6. **viscerally** instinctively

7. **tedious** boring; tiring

Wolfe: Well look at the times we're living in! Look at the city we're living in! The other day, they found a body on the cliff back there. Patrick was going, "My brother . . . .," and there were the little orange police markers of a body back there. I'd love to live in a world of tinky, tinky, tinky, isn't it all lovely, man? But that's not my world or the stakes of our landscape, and Shakespeare understood that. Over time, this writer, because he was so brilliant and so extraordinary, has been deified,[8] so that he's no longer about the human condition, but about the art. But art is created to express things human beings are incapable of expressing—Shakespeare's language gives eloquence to these complicated places that we live.

Newsday: How heretical[9] or subversive[10] is George's thinking to the RSC mindset, Patrick?

Stewart: Oh, George may not want to hear this, but I have a feeling that he would fit beautifully and brilliantly right into that world in Stratford-on-Avon. Not for long, mind you . . .

Wolfe: Who would drive who away?

Stewart: No, I think it would be incredibly thrilling for you to work with that company, but I can't see you settling into an eight-year contract. There is something appropriately anarchic[11] about George's rehearsal atmosphere and I can only say that was exactly what I needed right now . . . I've laughed so much these last six weeks. I've never had so much fun rehearsing Shakespeare as rehearsing this play. I certainly haven't laughed as much, ever.

---

8. **deified** made a god of; worshipped
9. **heretical** unorthodox; different
10. **subversive** revolutionary
11. **anarchic** chaotic; lacking order

Sylvan Barnet

The Tempest on the Stage

Sylvan Barnet describes various productions of The Tempest *since Shakespeare's day and discusses the different ways dramatists and actors have portrayed Caliban.*

These our actors,
As I foretold you, were all spirits and
Are melted into air, into thin air.

ALTHOUGH performances of plays are illusive[1] and elusive,[2] we do have some evidence about even the earliest productions of Shakespeare—for instance in original stage directions—and we have detailed descriptions of many later productions.

Shakespeare's company played chiefly at the Globe Theatre, an open-air playhouse that served the London public, and although there is every likelihood that *The Tempest* was produced there, in fact no document specifies that it was. The earliest reference to a performance tells us that the *The Tempest* was given before King James I on November 1, 1611, at the Banqueting House in Whitehall. The second reference (May 20, 1613) is to yet another performance at court, asserting that the play was staged as part of the wedding celebrations of Princess Elizabeth, daughter of Charles I. Court performances, especially performances of the highly allegorical dramatic works called masques, customarily made great use of spectacular effects, some of which would be particularly suited to *The Tempest*. Consider, for example, descriptions of nautical effects. Ben Jonson's *Masque of Blackness*, staged in the Banqueting House in 1605, began when a curtain decorated with a landscape painting dropped to the floor (the hall was not equipped to elevate the curtain): "An artificial sea was seen to shoot forth,

1. **illusive** deceptive or unreal
2. **elusive** difficult to explain

. . . raised with waves which seemed to move, and in some places the billow to break." Jonson's next production at court, *Masque of Beauty* (1608), required an "island floating on a calm water. . . ." *The Tempest* itself in some ways resembles a masque, and Prospero stages what is in effect a masque, when in IV.i.118ff. he conjures up Iris, Ceres, and Juno in "a most majestic vision." An original stage direction says that Juno "descends," but this action would cause no difficulty even at the Globe, which was equipped to let a deity[3] descend in a throne from above the stage. Still, perhaps when *The Tempest* was staged at court some visual effects were heightened or added. For instance, a production in the Banqueting House would have used artificial illumination, making possible lighting effects that could not have been achieved at the open-air Globe Theatre and that perhaps could not have been equaled even in the indoors Blackfriars Theatre used by Shakespeare's company in the winter. On the other hand, nothing specified in *The Tempest* was beyond the facilities available at the Globe.

Whatever the original productions were like, we can roughly classify most subsequent productions as either plain or fancy, that is, either relatively simply staged productions of the text or, on the other hand, relatively elaborately staged productions of a text altered to accommodate the machinery necessary to produce spectacular effects. Justifications can be offered for both kinds. Briefly, advocates of fancy, spectacular productions point to the court records we have just noticed, and argue that the production of *The Tempest* must have resembled other court productions. Advocates of plain production, on the other hand, argue that the records merely record but do not describe productions of *The Tempest*, and, moreover, that *The Tempest* was surely not written simply to be produced only twice at court. Shakespeare must have written the play for regular production at the Globe (though, again, there are no extant[4] references to any production there).

This much can certainly be said, based on the evidence of the stage directions in the first printed version of the play . . . Shakespeare valued auditory and visual effects. Thus, the play begins with "Thunder and lightning," and a little later in the first scene we encounter a stage direction that says, "Enter mariners wet." In the next scene Prospero says to Ariel, "Go make thyself like a nymph o' th' sea. Be subject / To no sight but thine and mine, invisible / To every eyeball else," and a few lines later we get this stage direction: "Enter Ariel like a water nymph." If Ariel is "invisible to every eyeball" other than Prospero's and Ariel's, why the costume of a sea nymph? Because, obviously, Shakespeare wanted to feast the spectators' eyes with

---

3. **deity** god

4. **extant** existing

unusual visual material. Later (III.iii.52) we get a stage direction calling for spectacle and magic: "Thunder and lightning. Enter Ariel, like a harpy;[5] claps his wings upon the table; and with a quaint device the banquet vanishes." Although a later stage direction calls for "Shapes" to enter and carry out the table, thus indicating that only the food on the table vanishes, not the table itself, the effect nevertheless must have been wonderful, and whatever the "quaint device" was—perhaps a table whose top flipped over—we seem to be in a world of masquelike machinery. Less complex, but no less indicative of Shakespeare's use of visual effects, is the stage direction at the beginning of the last act: "Enter Prospero in his magic robes." It seems reasonable to assume that these robes were something extraordinary.

Fancy versions of *The Tempest* were common in the late seventeenth century, and in the first half of the eighteenth. "Versions" is perhaps too generous; these adaptations were so extensive that they should be considered independent works rather than productions of Shakespeare's play. In 1667 William Davenant's and John Dryden's *The Tempest: or the Enchanted Island* was staged, a play which added (to balance Miranda) Hippolito, a handsome young man who had never seen a woman. There were other additions, too: Miranda was given a younger sister, Dorinda, who would marry Hippolito; Caliban was also given a sister, Sycorax; and Ariel was paired with a female sprite,[6] Milcha, who was pursued by two new comic sailors. Other changes included a good many cuts, especially in Prospero's lines. Shakespeare's play was thus made more symmetrical—more orderly, so to speak—and at the same time more fanciful, thus suiting the taste of an age that regarded itself as rational or classical and also as willing to enjoy the most extreme flights of a poet's imagination.

In 1674 Thomas Shadwell, adapting the adaptation, converted the piece into an opera. He added songs, a chorus of devils, and ballets of winds and Tritons, and in 1695 this opera was done with music by Henry Purcell. But the Davenant-Dryden version, too, continued to be immensely popular. It was produced at the Theatre Royal, Drury Lane, almost every year between 1701 and 1756, virtually driving Shakespeare's play from the stage. In 1745–46, however, Shakespeare's original play was given six performances at Drury Lane, and though the Davenant-Dryden version was again revived, its days were numbered. In 1757 David Garrick put on Shakespeare's play, cutting only 432 lines and (more remarkable, in an age that felt free to "improve" Shakespeare) adding only 14. Although this relatively faithful version of Shakespeare's play was regularly staged during much of the rest of the

5. **harpy** birdlike monster with human head and body

6. **sprite** small, mischievious supernatural being

eighteenth century, in 1787 John Philip Kemble, the noted classical actor, restored Hippolito and Dorinda. Because Dorinda's role was larger than Miranda's, it was much preferred by the actresses in the last decade of the century. Operatic treatments, too, continued in the early nineteenth century, but in 1838 William Charles Macready, manager of Covent Garden, played Prospero in a text remarkably close to Shakespeare's. Still, it should be noted that although Macready rejected the accretions,[7] his production employed a good deal of machinery, beginning with a huge ship, and continuing with Ariel flying around.

Charles Kean's production in 1857, which cut much of Shakespeare's text, was remarkable for its mechanically contrived spectacular effects, especially the storm and the other magic. It was boasted of this production: "The scenic appliances are of a more extensive nature than have been attempted in any theater in Europe." But whereas Davenant and Dryden believed that they had to refine Shakespeare's rather primitive plays for a more sophisticated age, the Victorian and Edwardian producers could with some reason believe they were fulfilling Shakespeare's intention when they provided as much splendor and magic as the theater (equipped with gaslight in 1817, and with limelight twenty years later) could produce. When electricity was introduced, in the third quarter of the nineteenth century, even more wonderful illusions became possible. This was an age when the theaters concentrated on splendid visual effects, and if the effects went far beyond anything that was possible in Shakespeare's own day it can nevertheless be argued that Shakespeare, with his thunder and lightning, his unusual costumes for Ariel and for Prospero, his masque of goddesses, and even his "wet" mariners, had himself sought to provide both realism and marvelous spectacles.

Probably the most notable Edwardian spectacular production was staged by Herbert Beerbohm Tree in 1904, when Tree played Caliban. An amazingly realistic shipwreck, in the Kean tradition, was followed by a blackout, then by the expository[8] scene between Prospero and Miranda, and then by a scene, behind a gauze, of nymphs in a purple light playing on the water (they were suspended by wires) and on the sand. The light gradually turned amber, and the sands became gold, to the strains of "Come unto These Yellow Sands." Tree transposed some scenes, and made some heavy cuts, reducing the last act to less than half of its original length, but he added elaborate pantomimes.[9] Thus, he deleted the material that follows Prospero's speech beginning "Ye elves of hills, brooks, standing lakes, and groves"

7. **accretions** additions
8. **expository** explanatory
9. **pantomimes** charades

(V.i.33–57), in which Prospero breaks his staff and vows to drown his book. Tree then added lightning, thunder, another vision of nymphs singing about their yellow sands, and a final pantomime. In a souvenir playbill Tree describes the end:

> Caliban creeps from his cave, and watches the departing ship bearing away the freight of humanity which for a brief spell has gladdened and saddened his island home, and taught him to "seek for grace." For the last time Ariel appears, singing the song of the bee. . . . The voice of the sprite rises higher and higher until it is merged into the note of the lark—Ariel is now as free as a bird. Caliban listens for the last time to the sweet air, then turns sadly in the direction of the departing ship. The play is ended. As the curtain rises again, the ship is seen on the horizon, Caliban stretching out his arms towards it in mute despair. The night falls, and Caliban is left on the lonely rock. He is a King once more.

But if most nineteenth-century productions strove to make Shakespeare real by means of elaborate sets and illusionistic lighting effects, the period also saw the rise of a counter-movement. As early as 1811 Ludwig Tieck, the German critic and translator of Shakespeare, pleaded for an Elizabethan-like theater in which the plays could be staged as they had been staged in Shakespeare's day. In 1894 William Poel founded the Elizabethan Stage Society, dedicated to restoring Elizabethan stage conditions. Poel saw that the use of cumbersome sets (encouraged by the proscenium[10] stage) destroyed the continuity of Shakespeare's scenes; since elaborate sets could not be quickly struck, directors tended to delete or transpose scenes that in the text intervened between scenes requiring a given massive set. Moreover, Poel believed that attempts at illusionism were futile. In 1897 he staged *The Tempest* on what was thought to be an Elizabethan stage erected in the hall of the Mansion House. Bernard Shaw, in a review of the production, gives us a good idea of Poel's aims:

> Mr. Poel says frankly, "See that singers' gallery up there! Well, let's pretend that it's the ship." We agree; and the thing is done. But how could we agree to such a pretence with a stage ship? Before it we should say, "Take that thing away: if our imagination is to create a ship, it must not be contradicted by something that apes a ship so vilely as to fill us with denial and repudiation[11] of its imposture."[12] The singing gallery

---

10. **proscenium** part of stage in front of the curtain
11. **repudiation** refusal
12. **imposture** deception

makes no attempt to impose on use: it disarms criticism by unaffected submission to the facts of the case, and throws itself honestly on our fancy, with instant success.

Poel dressed his players in Elizabethan costume, basing Prospero's costume on a print in a renaissance book about magic, and basing the costumes for the magical "Shapes" on prints illustrating court masques. He made some cuts—notably the bawdry[13]—but because the stage itself provided a permanent set, and because the spectators were expected to imagine the locales, he did not have to cut scenes that otherwise, requiring a change of set, would have been deleted. Poel's efforts to present Shakespeare without illusion were to have an enormous effect on the staging of Shakespeare, but they did not immediately banish Victorian spectacular, illusionistic productions. As we have seen, one of the most spectacular, Tree's, was given in 1904.

It is worth noting, by the way, that Tree played Caliban. This role has, of course, been played in several ways, sometimes as a drunken beast, sometimes as a noble savage, sometimes as the missing link (an 1890s interpretation based on Darwinism), and, recently, as a detribalized victim of colonial power. In the late seventeenth century, and in the eighteenth, Caliban was chiefly a minor comic figure, but with the rise of Romanticism he could become a "natural" man, a creature of sensibility. In 1806, in Kemble's production, he was not only a comic lout[14] but also a pitiful victim; in 1811–12, Samuel Taylor Coleridge, in a series of lectures, spoke of Caliban as a "noble being; a man in the sense of the imagination, all the images he utters are drawn from nature, and are highly poetical." A viewer of Macready's production of 1838 saw in Caliban one who "arouses our sympathies" because he resists a tyrannical oppressor. The late nineteenth-century Darwinian versions persisted into the first third of the twentieth century, in their way helping to make Caliban sympathetic, for, though a beast, he supposedly aspired to become a man. Beerbohm Tree, calling attention to Caliban's "love of music and his affinity with the unseen world," said that in Caliban "we discern in the soul which inhabits this elemental man the germs of a sense of beauty, in the dawn of art."

In our own time, Caliban has been variously presented—for example, as an American Indian, as a militant black, and (in Peter Brook's production at Stratford-upon-Avon in 1963 and especially in his production at the Round House in London in 1968) as a prehistoric man. . . . In a production at the Mermaid Theatre in London, in 1970, Jonathan Miller, advancing a

---

13. **bawdry** obscene language

14. **lout** awkward, stupid person

view that could not have been imagined before the middle of our century, saw the play as being about the destructive effects of colonialism, and he therefore depicted Caliban (played by a black actor) as the uneducated field hand, juxtaposed against Ariel (also played by a black actor), the cunning house slave. Prospero, of course, was the brutal local governor. (In 1945 in the United States, by the way, Canada Lee became the first black actor to play Caliban, but the production did not advance a view about colonialism.) Miller dressed his courtiers in black and introduced an attendant dwarf, thus evoking the world of Velasquez, i.e., the world of the Spanish conquistadores.[15] Miller has said that the underlying idea is the tragic destruction consequent upon a white assault on a tribal culture. Gone was Beerbohm Tree's Caliban, who at the end extended his hands toward the departing ship "in mute despair"; instead, Miller's *Tempest* ended with Caliban shaking his fist in rage, and Ariel—ever the alert opportunist—picking up the staff that their master had abandoned. But this view already shows signs of having worn thin; several productions in the last decade have returned to Caliban the noble savage, and, on the other hand, to Caliban as part of Prospero's own passionate (or even monstrous) nature.

Probably the most memorable Prospero of modern times has been John Gielgud, who has performed the role in four productions: 1930, 1940, 1957, and 1974. The last two productions especially evoked comment. The scenery in the 1957 production at Stratford-upon-Avon, and later at Drury Lane, directed by Peter Brook, was on the whole bleak, though some scenes showed a stifling tropical jungle. There was lots of magic—trapdoors and dissolving gauzes—but the masque was eerie rather than beautiful, and the costumes (except for Ferdinand's, which was orange, green, and white) were relatively drab. Except at the end, when he was again the duke, Gielgud wore not an elaborate magician's robe but a simple saronglike[16] garment. To several reviewers he was a haunted figure out of El Greco, a man filled with anguish, struggling to rise above the memory of the "high wrongs" he had endured. He finally conquered his passions, and, at the end, armed with a sword, set out for Milan, not as one who would live in easy retirement but as one who would continue to struggle against evil. In 1974, directed by Peter Hall at the National Theatre, Gielgud again played a Prospero whose mind was beating through most of the play, though the harshness (which Brook wanted in 1957) was somewhat modified by the music of the great organ voice for which Gielgud is famous, and the settings were magical and dreamlike. At the end of this version, when he appeared not in silks but in ordinary Elizabethan attire, the audience perceived a resemblance to

---

15. **conquistadores** conquerors

16. **saronglike** skirtlike outer garment

Shakespeare. In other ways, too, Hall sought to emphasize the Renaissance origin of the work. The production employed Inigo Jones-like symbolism: half of Caliban's face was monstrous, the other half that of the noble savage, and the stage balanced Prospero's cave (civilization) against Caliban's (primitivism).

Tad Williams

from *Caliban's Hour*

Tad Williams's portrayal of Caliban provides an example of an imaginative reworking of Shakespeare's story.

PROSPERO HELD himself a good man who had been poorly used. Even should we set aside his vicious treatment of me, Miranda, does putting the terror of a watery death into his enemies—achieved at what he felt was the petty cost of drowning a few dozen sailors—sound like the action of a good man? Does baiting with his daughter's virtue a snare to recatch his dukedom sound like goodness? And the selling of that daughter to his old enemy to enable his own resumption of power? I am sure you thought your swift love for Ferdinand genuine, but it was the last thing needed for Prospero's complete triumph: he must have known, even planned, that it would happen. How could you fail to love a tall, handsome young stranger? What comparison did you have but crippled, muddy Caliban?

The king's ship came to the island, lured and then sunk by some sorcery of your father and his hellish servant—a spell long in preparation, swift and terrifying in execution.

I knew nothing of it, but as Ariel worked its magics, painting storms across the sky that seemed to roar like a thousand monsters and scorch the very fabric of heaven, I hid cowering in a grotto[1] by the seashore, and was almost drowned there by the high-leaping waves. Had that happened, perhaps you would be smiling and dandling[2] your children even this moment, soothing their night terrors instead of facing one of your own. Certainly no tears would have been wasted on Caliban: by the time old Alonso and his

1. **grotto** cave
2. **dandling** pampering

liegemen[3] were drawn to the island, I had already served my purpose. But I escaped the waves and fought my way up the cliff face into the hills above, weeping in fear as the thunder cracked on, louder than any I had ever heard. On either side of me trees were split by jagged lightning thrusts and left as smoking husks,[4] a hundred replicas of the riven[5] pine from which Ariel had sprung.

Thus I did not see the ship's survivors coming to land. When the first of them happened upon me, I was astonished, and thought them spirits of the storm, perhaps even brothers to Ariel. I cowered in the undergrowth beside the path, but they were as frightened by me as I of them.

Poor Stephano and Trinculo. Unlucky men, to have made such a doomful friend as me!

Oh, the lies your father later told you, Miranda, and which you hurried to believe. He told you that those sailors and I plotted some murderous rebellion, that only his wits and Ariel's magics saved you and him from death. Lies, lies, lies!

They were rough fellows, those two, but honest withal. When I spoke, thinking to placate[6] these new tormentors, they thought me a prodigy, a sport of nature. *An ape that speaks!* one said, and the other nodded. When I told them I was the son of an exile, and that I had been enslaved by a later arrival, they were astounded, but when I told them who it was who had enslaved me they were less surprised.

Prospero the warlock. That name is well-known, and well-feared, said Stephano. *His dark arts were a danger to Milan, and so he was driven out.*

Then they feared for the safety of their king, who had earned Prosper's hatred by supporting the wizard's brother in his overthrow. They had been sent to explore the island and find help if possible, but now they gave over their task and hurried back toward the beach where the ship's passengers had floundered ashore, bidding me accompany them and promising me food and protection from my master. For the first time, I dared to hope that my life might be changed.

Hope is a cruelty even Ariel had not mastered. Foolish Caliban. Foolish, foolish mud-man!

The king and his party were gone, the beach empty but for a single sandy corpse, one of the sailors cast overboard by the storm who had finally washed onto the shore. I stared at his bulging, sightless eyes as Stephano and Trinculo cursed their luck. He was another of your father's victims,

---

3. **liegemen** faithful followers
4. **husks** outer shells
5. **riven** split
6. **placate** soothe

Miranda. I do not even know his name, but he had curly dark hair and wore a cross carved from ivory around his neck. In some other world I may see him, and if so, I will tell him that there is no justice on this earth, where the games of some cause the deaths of men they do not know.

I have not spent long among your kind, Miranda. Perhaps he knew this even before the sea took him.

We hurried on in pursuit of King Alonso, but Ariel's storm-spell had left webs of magic everywhere; my familiar island had become a maze of confusion. False trails, misleading sounds, and sourceless lights, several times a shimmer of music from nowhere, led us through the forest tracks for hours, but never any closer to our goal. We grew tired and dropped for a while to sleep a fitful sleep before wakening and staggering on.

We arrived at the house on the hillside at last, to discover that the game was played, the story told, and we three but comic afterthoughts. Ariel laid a further spell on Stephano and Trinculo that made their weariness seem drunken foolery, thus to discredit their warnings. King Alonso, bemused by your father's magics, had made a great apology and renunciation,[7] and now stood beaming like a drunkard himself, clasping Prospero's hand and proclaiming that all wrongs would be righted, all crimes punished. And since Antonio, your father's usurping[8] brother, had been one of those drowned, there was conveniently no other claimant to Milan's throne.

But even as I swayed, blinking at what for me was an almost incomprehensibly vast crowd of other people, something I had never thought to see, I began to realize that the wrongs I had suffered would go very much unrighted.

Then you appeared, Miranda, clutching at a boy with a face pale as goat's milk, and an expression no cleverer than would adorn a goat's front. But it was not the expression on *his* face that caused my heart to tumble down into a dark hole.

The king had apparently thought his cream-faced son dead, and made loud cries of astonishment. He embraced him, then, wonderingly, embraced you as well.

This is my Miranda, his son Ferdinand told him. *She will be my wife. She is beautiful and kind, and is properly a maiden.*

Your daughter, Duke Prosper? Alonso asked in some surprise.

Aye, and pure, every inch, answered your father. *Fit bride for a prince. If it is your pleasure they should wed, we may make the return voyage a wedding-progress.*

Alas, declared Alonso, *our ship is sunk. We are marooned, all.*

Prospero nodded, smiling deep in his beard.

---

7. **renunciation** denial

8. **usurping** infringing; meddling

There was other talk then, but I did not hear it. The sight of you mooning at Ferdinand was a knife in my eye. My ears filled with a terrible rushing, as though Ariel had re-summoned the storm; I fell to my knees between Stephano and Trinculo and gave out a great cry. But no one paid any attention. The spell-dazzled pair beside me had not the wits, and all the others were too full of questions and celebration. I groaned again, and would not have been surprised had my heart split in my breast and killed me. But Fate had in mind for me a longer spell of suffering.

There was a great festival that night. Ariel conjured a magic banquet, but with freedom only hours away, I wonder how much attention the hell-sprite gave to its work: some of the viands[9] turned ghostly and then vanished entirely before they could be eaten. As for the rest of the meal, one might wonder how filling it was.

In any case, it all mattered little to me. Prospero bade me serve, but I would not. After Stephano and Trinculo had been called rebels and clapped in chains by their ungrateful ruler, I no longer cared what might happen, and lay all evening as one dead near the front door of the house, refusing to get up. Prospero was angry, but did not have Ariel harry[10] me into service. Perhaps he feared to show his new allies how his will was usually accomplished.

You, Miranda, you had eyes for nothing but your new love, that odious[11] princeling with whom, I suspect, your father had long planned to breed you like a heifer. Ferdinand paddled at your neck and fed you with his own fingers—an affection that I have no doubt lasted only slightly longer than Ariel's repast[12]—while your sire looked on, beaming his approval. Your father's onetime toady[13] Gonzalo, now restored to his service, proposed salutation after salutation, both to Prospero and Alonso, bidding Heaven smile on the binding-up of old hurts and the union of two such noble families.

And they all stand upon my neck, I groaned in the shadows. *Ban, Ban, Caliban.*

At the end of the meal, Ariel—still invisible to any save me and Prospero, since you had eyes only for Prince Whey-face—flew into the sky at you father's whispered command.

Behold, your father cried aloud. *The last of my magics, but not the least!* He waved his staff.

Instantly there flew across the face of the moon a streak of fire, which widened into a blazing sheet, then became the image of a ship. The king's

---

9. **viands** choice foods; delicacies

10. **harry** force

11. **odious** detestable

12. **repast** feast

13. **toady** flatterer

vessel, etched in lines of flame, burned against the velvety night, rocking and wallowing as though it might sink.

Miracle of miracles, cried Alonso, *it is the very picture of the tempest that wrecked us!*

The fiery boat sank in burning waves and tiny flaming figures swam away from it. Then, as the onlookers gasped and pointed, the ship faded in a drizzle of sparks. It was only when the last of the glowing drops had vanished that we could see a great shimmer of light rising above the trees, a subtler radiance that seemed to have its source in the ocean far below us.

What is this, Duke Prosperso? cried young Ferdinand, clasping you to him with a great show of protectiveness. *Have your fire-magics set the forest ablaze?*

After me and you will discover, your father said, and set out down the hillside, his staff suddenly burning at its tip like a torch.

The company rose and followed him. I would have remained where I lay huddled, having no desire to see anything more, half hoping that the forest had indeed caught fire and would soon burn me and the island and everyone else to mute ash. But of course, Ariel and Prospero intended that *all* should witness their final triumph, and I was soon chivvied[14] down the hill after the others, pursued by invisible biters.

We stopped upon the beach, all but me staring in awe at the ocean, which shone from below with a great pearly green light, as though the absent sun were reborn in its depths. The glow spread. Then, with a great tumult of waters, the king's true ship rose up through the fathoms until it bobbed atop the waves. Seablood ran off it in great sheets. Blue fire leaped among the masts. Here and there a waxy corpse dangled in the rigging.

Your ship is raised, Prospero told the king, and bowed as one who has done a modest but significant favor. *We may sail back to Naples. Justly, I am once more become Milan absolute, and so I abjure*[15] *further magics.*

As he spoke, he scratched something in the sand—marks the others were too thunderstruck by the appearance of the ship to notice. But I, perhaps alone, heard a great buzzing peal of laughter echo across the strand, then saw some flaming thing leap from the pinnacle of the mainmast and vanish in a shower of yellow sparks. An instant later something hurtled past me, knocking me from my feet with the wind of its passage, leaving only the echo of a few mocking words behind as it flew to freedom.

Find a new master
Get a new man!

---

14. **chivvied** moved

15. **abjure** renounce or give up

As I lay panting in the dirt, you detached yourself from the milling company and made your way toward me. You were dressed in your finest clothes; I wore only rags and mud, my head garlanded with briar tangles.

Caliban?

I turned my face away.

My father is a strict man, but not a cruel one. I have told him that your rebellion was only foolishness. He has decided to forgive you.

I clenched my fist but said nothing. I wished only for you to go away and leave me in peace.

You will be punished no further. And you will have your island back again, as you wished, for we are returning to Naples with King Alonso.

You sensed the anger in my silence, for you said: *Can you not be happy for me, Caliban? I love Ferdinand truly, and soon I will see again the place I was born. It will be as a new world to me!*

I stared at the pale-faced, chattering company she had left down on the beach, vile Prospero, senile Alonso, and all the rest.

O, brave new world it must be, I growled, *that has such creatures in it. Go to it, you. It will be a fit place for your like.*

You turned away then, and until I appeared in your bedroom tonight, we exchanged no more words. But I was not to be allowed even my final furious mourning. As I crawled away into the forest, I heard footfalls behind me. Your father's black boots stepped in front of me, forcing me to halt.

I have dealt harshly with you in the past, Caliban, but it was for your own betterment. Now I leave you to your future, and your freedom.

Go away, you madman! I cried. *Let me be!*

He hesitated, then turned and paced back toward the beach. I crouched, sobbing, and heard him stop again. I lowered my head and tried to cover my ears, but could not shut out his last, terrible words.

In my way, little savage, I loved you once.

And then he was gone.

Silvester Jourdain

from *A Discovery of the Bermudas, Otherwise Called the Isle of Devils*

Shakespeare based The Tempest *on a shipwreck that occurred in 1609. This account, from 1610, was written by a passenger who survived the wreck.*

BEING in [a] ship called the "Sea Venture," with Sir Thomas Gates our governor, Sir George Somers, and Captain Newport, three most worthy, honored gentlemen (whose valor[1] and fortitude[2] the world must needs take notice of, and that in most honorable designs) bound for Virginia, in the height of 30 degrees of northerly latitude or thereabouts we were taken with a most sharp and cruel storm upon the five-and-twentieth day of July, anno[3] 1609, which did not only separate us from the residue of our fleet (which were eight in number), but with the violent working of the seas our ship became so shaken, torn, and leaked that she received so much water as covered two tier of hogsheads[4] above the ballast;[5] that our men stood up to the middles with buckets, barricos, and kettles to bail out the water and continually pumped for three days and three nights together without any intermission; and yet the water seemed rather to increase than to diminish. Insomuch that all our men, being utterly spent, tired, and disabled for longer labor, were even resolved, without any hope of their lives, to shut up

1. **valor** courage
2. **fortitude** courage or strength of mind in the face of pain, danger, or adversity
3. **anno** year
4. **hogshead** large barrel
5. **ballast** material that maintains a boat's stability

the hatches and to have committed themselves to the mercy of the sea (which is said to be merciless), or rather to the mercy of their mighty God and redeemer (whose mercies exceed all His works), seeing no help nor hope in the apprehension of man's reason that any mother's child would escape that inevitable danger, which every man had proposed and digested to himself, of present sinking. So that some of them, having some good and comfortable waters in the ship, fetched them and drunk one to the other, taking their last leave one of the other until their more joyful and happy meeting in a more blessed world; when it pleased God out of His most gracious and merciful providence so to direct and guide our ship (being left to the mercy of the sea) for her most advantage that Sir George Somers (sitting upon the poop[6] of the ship, where he sate three days and three nights together, without meal's meat and [with] little or no sleep), conning[7] the ship to keep her as upright as he could (for otherwise she must needs instantly have foundered), most wishedly-happily descried land. Whereupon he most comfortably encouraged the company to follow their pumping and by no means to cease bailing out of the water with their buckets, barricos, and kettles; whereby they were so overwearied, and their spirits so spent with long fasting and continuance of their labor, that for the most part they were fallen asleep in corners and wheresoever they chanced first to sit or lie; but, hearing news of land, wherewith they grew to be somewhat revived, being carried with will and desire beyond their strength, every man bustled up and gathered his strength and feeble spirits together to perform as much as their weak force would permit him; through which weak means it pleased God to work so strongly as the water was stayed for that little time (which, as we all much feared, was the last period of our breathing) and the ship kept from present sinking, when it pleased God to send her within half an English mile of that land that Sir George Somers had not long before descried, which were the islands of the Bermudas.

And there neither did our ship sink but, more fortunately in so great a misfortune, fell in between two rocks, where she was fast lodged and locked for further budging; whereby we gained not only sufficient time, with the present help of our boat and skiff,[8] safely to set and convey our men ashore (which were 150 in number) but afterwards had time and leisure to save some good part of our goods and provision, which the water had not spoiled, with all the tacking of the ship and much of the iron about her, which were necessaries not a little available[9] for the building and furnishing of a new

6. **poop** stern of a ship

7. **conning** keeping a lookout and directing the steersman

8. **skiff** rowboat

9. **available** advantageous

ship and pinnace,[10] which we made there for the transporting and carrying of us to Virginia. But our delivery was not more strange, in falling so opportunely and happily upon the land, as our feeding and preservation was beyond our hopes and all men's expectations most admirable.[11]

For the islands of the Bermudas, as every man knoweth that hath heard or read of them, were never inhabited by any Christian or heathen people but ever esteemed and reputed a most prodigious and enchanted place, affording nothing but gusts, storms, and foul weather, which made every navigator and mariner to avoid them as Scylla and Charybdis, or as they would shun the Devil himself; and no man was ever heard to make for the place but as, against their wills, they have by storms and dangerousness of the rocks, lying seven leagues unto the sea, suffered shipwreck. Yet did we find there the air so temperate and the country so abundantly fruitful of all fit necessaries for the sustentation[12] and preservation of man's life that, most in a manner of all our provisions of bread, beer, and victual[13] being quite spoiled in lying long drowned in salt water, notwithstanding we were there for the space of nine months (few days over or under) not only well received, comforted, and with good satiety[14] contented, but out of the abundance thereof provided us some reasonable quantity and proportion of provision to carry us for Virginia and to maintain ourselves and that company we found there, to the great relief of them, as it fell out, in their so great extremities and, in respect of the shortness of time, until it pleased God that by My Lord's coming thither[15] their store was better supplied. And greater and better provisions we might have made if we had had better means for the storing and transportation thereof. Wherefore my opinion sincerely of this island is that whereas it hath been and is still accounted the most dangerous, infortunate, and most forlorn place of the world, it is in truth the richest, health-fullest, and pleasing land (the quantity and bigness thereof considered) and merely natural, as ever man set foot upon. The particular profits and benefits whereof shall be more especially inserted and hereunto annexed, which every man to his own private knowledge, that was there, can avouch[16] and justify for a truth.

Upon the eight-and-twentieth day of July, 1609 (after the extremity of

---

10. **pinnace** small boat
11. **admirable** wonderful
12. **sustentation** livelihood
13. **victual** supplies; food
14. **satiety** fullness
15. **thither** to
16. **avouch** acknowledge

the storm was something qualified), we fell upon the shore at the Bermudas; where after our general, Sir Thomas Gates, Sir George Somers, and Captain Newport had by their provident carefulness landed all their men and so much of the goods and provisions out of the ship as was not utterly spoiled, every man disposed and applied himself to search for and to seek out such relief and sustentation as the country afforded. And Sir George Somers, a man inured[17] to extremities (and knowing what thereunto belonged) was in this service neither idle nor backward but presently by his careful industry went and found out sufficient of many kind of fishes, and so plentiful thereof that in half an hour he took so many great fishes with hooks as did suffice the whole company one day. And fish is there so abundant that if a man step into the water they will come round about him; so that men were fain to get out for fear of biting. These fishes are very fat and sweet and of that proportion and bigness that three of them will conveniently lade[18] two men: those we called rockfish. Besides there are such abundance of mullets[19] that with a seine[20] might be taken at one draught[21] one thousand at the least; and infinite store of pilchards;[22] with divers kinds of great fishes, the names of them unknown to me; of crayfishes very great ones and so great store as that there hath been taken in one night with making lights even sufficient to feed the whole company a day. The country affordeth great abundance of hogs, as that there hath been taken by Sir George Somers, who was the first hunted for them to the number of two-and-thirty at one time, which he brought to the company in a boat built by his own hands.

There is fowl in great num[ber] upon the islands where they breed, that there hath been taken in two or three hours a thousand at the least, the bird being of the bigness of a good pigeon and layeth eggs as big as hen eggs upon the sand, where they come and lay them daily although men sit down amongst them, that there hath been taken up in one morning by Sir Thomas Gates's men one thousand of eggs; and Sir George Somers' men, coming a little distance of time after them, have stayed there whilst they came and laid their eggs amongst them, that they brought away as many more with them, with many young birds very fat and sweet.

Another seafowl there is that lieth in little holes in the ground, like unto a cony[23] hole, and are in great numbers, exceeding good meat, very fat

---

17. **inured** accustomed
18. **lade** fill up
19. **mullets** kind of fish
20. **seine** fishing net
21. **draught** draft
22. **pilchards** small fish
23. **cony** rabbit

and sweet (those we had in the winter) and their eggs are white and of that bigness that they are not to be known from hen eggs. The other bird's eggs are speckled and of a different color. There are also great store and plenty of herons, and those so familiar and tame that we beat them down from the trees with stones and staves—but such were young herons—besides many white herons without so much as a black or grey feather on them; with other small birds so tame and gentle that, a man walking in the woods with a stick and whistling to them, they will come and gaze on you, so near that you may strike and kill many of them with your stick; and with singing and holloing you may do the like.

There are also great store of tortoises (which some call turtles) and those so great that I have seen a bushel of eggs in one of their bellies, which are sweeter than any hen egg; and the tortoise itself is all very good meat and yieldeth great store of oil, which is as sweet as any butter; and one of them will suffice fifty men a meal, at the least; and of these hath been taken great store, with two boats, at the least forty in one day.

The country yieldeth divers fruits, as prickled pears, great abundance, which continue green upon the trees all the year; also great plenty of mulberries, white and red, and on the same are great store of silkworms, which yield cods of silk, both white and yellow, being some coarse and some fine.

And there is a tree called a palmetto tree, which hath a very sweet berry upon which the hogs do most feed; but our men, finding the sweetness of them, did willingly share with the hogs for them, they being very pleasant and wholesome, which made them careless almost of any bread with their meat; which occasioned us to carry in a manner all that store of flour and meal we did or could save for Virginia. The head of the palmetto tree is very good meat, either raw or sodden; it yieldeth a head which weigheth about twenty pound and is far better meat than any cabbage.

There are an infinite number of cedar trees (the fairest, I think, in the world) and those bring forth a very sweet berry and wholesome to eat.

The country (forasmuch as I could find myself or hear by others) affords no venomous creature, or so much as a rat or mouse or any other thing unwholesome.

There is great store of pearl, and some of them very fair, round, and oriental,[24] and you shall find at least one hundred seed of pearl in one oyster. There hath been likewise found some good quantity of ambergris,[25] and that of the best sort. There are also great plenty of whales, which I conceive are very easy to be killed, for they come so usually and ordinarily to the shore

---

24. oriental used here to mean lustrous

25. ambergris waxy substance formed in the intestines of sperm whales, used in making perfume

that we heard them oftentimes in the night abed and have seen many of them near the shore in the daytime.

There was born upon the Bermudas, at the time of our being there, two children, the one a man-child, there baptized by the name of Bermudas, and a woman-child, baptized by the name of Bermuda; as also there was a marriage between two English people upon the island. This island, I mean the main island, with all the broken islands adjacent, are made in the form of a half moon, but a little more rounder, and divided into many broken islands, and there are many good harbors in it; but we could find [only] one especial place to go in, or rather to go out from it, which was not altogether free from some danger, and that lieth on the southeast side, where there is three fathoms water at the entrance thereof, but within six, seven, or eight fathoms at the least, where you may safely be landlocked from the danger of all winds and weathers, and more to the trees. The coming into it is so narrow and strait between the rocks as that it will with small store of munition be fortified and easily defended with all advantage the place affords against the forces of the potentest king of Europe.

There are also plenty of hawks and very good tobacco, as I think, which through forgetfulness I had almost omitted.

Now, having finished and rigged our ship and pinnace, the one called the "Deliverance," the pinnace the "Patience," we prepared and made ourselves ready to ship for Virginia, having powdered[26] some store of hogs' flesh for provision thither and the company thereof for some reasonable time but were compelled to make salt there for the same purpose, for all our salt was spent and spoiled before we recovered the shore. We carried with us also a good portion of tortoise oil, which either for frying or baking did us very great pleasure, it being very sweet, nourishing, and wholesome.

The greatest defects we found there was tar and pitch for our ship and pinnace, instead whereof we were forced to make lime there of a hard kind of stone and use it, which for the present occasion and necessity, with some wax we found cast up by the sea from some shipwreck, served the turn to pay[27] the seams of the pinnace Sir George Somers built, for which he had neither pitch nor tar.

So that God, in the supplying of all our wants beyond all measure, showed Himself still merciful unto us, that we might accomplish our intended voyage to Virginia, for which I confidently hope He doth yet reserve a blessing in store, and to the which I presume every honest and religious heart will readily give their Amen.

---

26. **powdered** salted

27. **to pay** cover with tar or the like

When all things were made ready and commodiously[28] fitted, the wind coming fair, we set sail and put off from the Bermudas the tenth of May in the year 1610, and arrived at Jamestown in Virginia the four-and-twentieth day of the same month, where we found some three-score persons living.

28. **commodiously** amply

Mark Twain

from *Is Shakespeare Dead?*

Whether or not Shakespeare wrote all of the plays that he has been credited with is the subject of a long and enduring dispute. Famed author Mark Twain offers his opinion in the following reading.

A FRIEND HAS SENT me a new book, from England—*The Shakespeare Problem Restated*—well restated and closely reasoned; and my fifty years' interest in that matter—asleep for the last three years—is excited once more. It is an interest which was born of Delia Bacon's book—away back in that ancient day—1857, or maybe 1856. About a year later my pilot-master, Bixby, transferred me from his own steamboat to the *Pennsylvania*, and placed me under the orders and instructions of George Ealer—dead now, these many, many years. I steered for him a good many months—as was the humble duty of the pilot-apprentice: stood a daylight watch and spun the wheel under the severe superintendence and correction of the master. He was a prime chess player and an idolater[1] of Shakespeare. He would play chess with anybody; even with me, and it cost his official dignity something to do that. Also—quite uninvited—he would read Shakespeare to me; not just casually, but by the hour, when it was his watch, and I was steering. He read well, but not profitably for me, because he constantly injected commands into the text. That broke it all up, mixed it all up, tangled it all up—to that degree, in fact, that if we were in a risky and difficult piece of river an ignorant person couldn't have told, sometimes, which observations were Shakespeare's and which were Ealer's. For instance:

---

1. **idolater** worshiper

What man dare, *I* dare!

Approach thou *what* are you laying in the leads for? what . . . an idea! like the rugged ease her off a little, ease her off! rugged Russian bear, the armed rhinoceros or the *there* she goes! meet her, meet her! didn't you *know* she'd smell the reef if you crowded it like that? Hyrcan tiger; take any shape but that and my firm nerves she'll be in the *woods* the first you know! stop the starboard! come ahead strong on the larboard! back the starboard! . . . *Now* then, you're all right; come ahead on the starboard; straighten up and go 'long, never tremble: or be alive again, and dare me to the desert *damnation* can't you keep away from that greasy water? pull her down! snatch her! snatch her baldheaded! with thy sword; if trembling I inhabit then, lay in the leads!—no, only the starboard one, leave the other alone, protest me the baby of a girl. Hence horrible shadow! eight bells—that watchman's asleep again, I reckon, go down and call Brown yourself, unreal mockery, hence!"

He certainly was a good reader, and splendidly thrilling and stormy and tragic, but it was a damage to me, because I have never since been able to read Shakespeare in a calm and sane way. I cannot rid it of his explosive interlardings,[2] they break in everywhere with their irrelevant "What . . . are you up to *now!* pull her down! more! *more!*—there now, steady as you go," and the other disorganizing interruptions that were always leaping from his mouth. When I read Shakespeare now, I can hear them as plainly as I did in that long-departed time—fifty-one years ago. I never regarded Ealer's readings as educational. Indeed they were a detriment to me.

His contributions to the text seldom improved it, but barring that detail he was a good reader, I can say that much for him. He did not use the book, and did not need to; he knew his Shakespeare as well as Euclid ever knew his multiplication table.

Did he have something to say—this Shakespeare-adoring Mississippi pilot—anent[3] Delia Bacon's book? Yes. And he said it; said it all the time, for months—in the morning watch, the middle watch, the dog watch; and probably kept it going in his sleep. He bought the literature of the dispute as fast as it appeared, and we discussed it all through thirteen hundred miles of river four times traversed in every thirty-five days—the time required by that swift boat to achieve two round trips. We discussed, and discussed, and discussed, and disputed and disputed and disputed; at any rate *he* did, and I got in a word now and then when he slipped a cog[4] and there was a vacancy.

---

2. **interlardings** unrelated comments

3. **anent** concerning

4. **slipped a cog** missed a beat; paused

He did his arguing with heat, with energy, with violence; and I did mine with the reserve and moderation of a subordinate who does not like to be flung out of a pilot-house that is perched forty feet above the water. He was fiercely loyal to Shakespeare and cordially scornful of Bacon and of all the pretensions of the Baconians. So was I—at first. And at first he was glad that that was my attitude. There were even indications that he admired it; indications dimmed, it is true, by the distance that lay between the lofty boss-pilotical altitude and my lowly one, yet perceptible to me; perceptible, and translatable into a compliment—compliment coming down from above the snow-line and not well thawed in the transit, and not likely to set anything afire, not even a cub-pilot's self-conceit; still a detectable compliment, and precious.

Naturally it flattered me into being more loyal to Shakespeare—if possible—than I was before, and more prejudiced against Bacon—if possible—than I was before. And so we discussed and discussed, both on the same side, and were happy. For a while. Only for a while. Only for a very little while, a very very, very little while. Then the atmosphere began to change; began to cool off.

A brighter person would have seen what the trouble was, earlier than I did, perhaps, but I saw it early enough for all practical purposes. You see, he was of an argumentative disposition. Therefore it took him but a little time to get tired of arguing with a person who agreed with everything he said and consequently never furnished him a provocative to flare up and show what he could do when it came to clear, cold, hard, rose-cut, hundred-faceted, diamond-flashing *reasoning.* That was his name for it. It has been applied since, with complacency, as many as several times in the Bacon-Shakespeare scuffle. On the Shakespeare side.

Then the thing happened which has happened to more persons than to me when principle and personal interest found themselves in opposition to each other and a choice had to be made: I let principle go, and went over to the other side. Not the entire way, but far enough to answer the requirements of the case. That is to say, I took this attitude, to wit: I only *believed* Bacon wrote Shakespeare, whereas I *knew* Shakespeare didn't. Ealer was satisfied with that, and the war broke loose. Study, practice, experience in handling my end of the matter presently enabled me to take my new position almost seriously; a little bit later, utterly seriously; a little later still, lovingly, gratefully, devotedly; finally: fiercely, rabidly, uncompromisingly. After that, I was welded to my faith, I was theoretically ready to die for it, and I looked down with compassion not unmixed with scorn, upon everybody else's faith that didn't tally[5] with mine. That faith, imposed upon me

5. **tally** correspond

by self-interest in that ancient day, remains my faith to-day, and in it I find comfort, solace, peace, and never-failing joy. You see how curiously theological it is. . . .

Earler did a lot of our "reasoning"—not to say substantially all of it. The slaves of his cult have a passion for calling it by that large name. We others do not call our inductions and deductions and reductions by any name at all. They show for themselves, what they are, and we can with tranquil confidence leave the world to ennoble[6] them with a title of its own choosing.

Now and then when Earler had to stop to cough, I pulled my induction-talents together and hove[7] the controversial lead myself: always getting eight feet, eight-and-a-half, often nine, sometimes even quarter-less-twain—as *I* believed; but always, "no bottom," as *he* said.

I got the best of him only once. I prepared myself. I wrote out a passage from Shakespeare—it may have been the very one I quoted a while ago, I don't remember—and riddled it with his wild steamboatful interlardings. When an unrisky opportunity offered, one lovely summer day, when we had sounded and buoyed a tangled patch of crossings known as Hell's Half Acre, and were aboard again and he had sneaked the *Pennsylvania* triumphantly through it without once scraping sand, and the *A. T. Lacey* had followed in our wake and got stuck, and he was feeling good, I showed it to him. It amused him. I asked him to fire it off: *read* it; read it, I diplomatically added, as only *he* could read dramatic poetry. The compliment touched him where he lived. He did read it; read it with surpassing fire and spirit; read it as it will never be read again; for *he* knew how to put the right music into those thunderous interlardings and make them seem a part of the text, make them sound as if they were bursting from Shakespeare's own soul, each one of them a golden inspiration and not to be left out without damage to the massed and magnificent whole.

I waited a week, to let the incident fade; waited longer; waited until he brought up for reasonings and vituperation[8] my pet position, my pet argument, the one which I was fondest of, the one which I prized far above all others in my ammunition-wagon, to wit: that Shakespeare couldn't have written Shakespeare's works, for the reason that the man who wrote them was limitlessly familiar with the laws, and the law-courts, and law-proceedings, and lawyer-talk, and lawyer-ways—and if Shakespeare was possessed of the infinitely-divided star-dust that constituted this vast wealth, *how* did he get it, and *where*, and *when?*

"From books."

---

6. **ennoble** honor
7. **hove** said with effort
8. **vituperation** verbal abuse

From books! That was always the idea. I answered as my readings of the champions of my side of the great controversy had taught me to answer: that a man can't handle glibly[9] and easily and comfortably and successfully the *argot*[10] of a trade at which he has not personally served. He will make mistakes; he will not, and cannot, get the trade-phrasings precisely and exactly right; and the moment he departs, by even a shade, from a common trade-form, the reader who has served that trade will know the writer *hasn't*. Ealer would not be convinced; he said a man could learn how to correctly handle the subtleties and mysteries and free-masonries of *any* trade by careful reading and studying. But when I got him to read again the passage from Shakespeare with the interlardings, he perceived, himself, that books couldn't teach a student a bewildering multitude of pilot-phrases so thoroughly and perfectly that he could talk them off in book and play or conversation and make no mistake that a pilot would not immediately discover. It was a triumph for me. He was silent awhile, and I knew what was happening: he was losing his temper. And I knew he would presently close the session with the same old argument that was always his stay and his support in time of need; the same old argument, the one I couldn't answer—because I dasn't: the argument that I was an ass, and better shut up. He delivered it, and I obeyed.

Oh, dear, how long ago it was—how pathetically long ago! And here am I, old, forsaken, forlorn and alone, arranging to get that argument out of somebody again. . . .

For the instruction of the ignorant I will make a list, now, of those details of Shakespeare's history which are *facts*—verified facts, established facts, undisputed facts.

Facts

He was born on the 23d of April, 1564.

Of good farmer-class parents who could not read, could not write, could not sign their names.

At Stratford, a small back settlement which in that day was shabby and unclean, and densely illiterate. Of the nineteen important men charged with the government of the town, thirteen had to "make their mark" in attesting important documents, because they could not write their names.

Of the first eighteen years of his life *nothing* is known. They are a blank.

On the 27th of November (1582) William Shakespeare took out a license to marry Anne Whateley.

---

9. **glibly** smoothly

10. ***argot*** slang; vocabulary

Next day William Shakespeare took out a license to marry Anne Hathaway. She was eight years his senior.

William Shakespeare married Anne Hathaway. In a hurry. By grace of a reluctantly-granted dispensation there was but one publication of the banns.

Within six months the first child was born.

About two (blank) years followed, during which period *nothing at all happened to Shakespeare*, so far as anybody knows.

Then came twins—1585. February.

Two blank years follow.

Then—1587—he makes a ten-year visit to London, leaving the family behind.

Five blank years follow. During this period *nothing happened to him*, as far as anybody actually knows.

Then—1592—there is mention of him as an actor.

Next year—1593—his name appears in the official list of players.

Next year—1594—he played before the queen. A detail of no consequence: other obscurities did it every year of the forty-five of her reign. And remained obscure.

Three pretty full years follow. Full of play-acting. Then

In 1597 he bought New Place, Stratford.

Thirteen or fourteen busy years follow; years in which he accumulated money, and also reputation as actor and manager.

Meantime his name, liberally and variously spelt, had become associated with a number of great plays and poems, as (ostensibly) author of the same.

Some of these, in these years and later, were pirated, but he made no protest.

Then—1610–11—he returned to Stratford and settled down for good and all, and busied himself in lending money, trading in tithes, trading in land and houses; shirking a debt of forty-one shillings, borrowed by his wife during his long desertion of his family; suing debtors for shillings and coppers;[11] being sued himself for shillings and coppers; and acting as confederate to a neighbor who tried to rob the town of its rights in a certain common, and did not succeed.

---

11. **shillings and coppers** coins

He lived five or six years—till 1616—in the joy of these elevated pursuits. Then he made a will, and signed each of its three pages with his name.

A thoroughgoing business man's will. It named in minute detail every item of property he owned in the world—houses, lands, sword, silver-gilt bowl, and so on—all the way down to his "second-best bed" and its furniture.

It carefully and calculatingly distributed his riches among the members of his family, overlooking no individual of it. Not even his wife: the wife he had been enabled to marry in a hurry by urgent grace of a special dispensation before he was nineteen; the wife whom he had left husbandless so many years; the wife who had had to borrow forty-one shillings in her need, and which the lender was never able to collect of the prosperous husband, but died at last with the money still lacking. No, even this wife was remembered in Shakespeare's will.

He left her that "second-best bed."

And *not another thing;* not even a penny to bless her lucky widowhood with.

It was eminently[12] and conspicuously[13] a business man's will, not a poet's.

It mentioned *not a single book.*

Books were much more precious than swords and silver-gilt bowls and second-best beds in those days, and when a departing person owned one he gave it a high place in his will.

The will mentioned *not a play, not a poem, not an unfinished literary work, not a scrap of manuscript of any kind.*

Many poets have died poor, but this is the only one in history that has died this poor; the others all left literary remains behind. Also a book. Maybe two.

If Shakespeare had owned a dog—but we need not go into that: we know he would have mentioned it in his will. If a good dog, Susanna would have got it; if an inferior one his wife would have got a dower[14] interest in it. I wish he had had a dog, just so we could see how painstakingly he would have divided that dog among the family, in his careful business way.

He signed the will in three places.

In earlier years he signed two other official documents.

---

12. **eminently** grandly
13. **conspicuously** unmistakably
14. **dower** widow's inheritance

These five signatures still exist.

There are *no other specimens of his penmanship in existence*. Not a line.

Was he prejudiced against the art? His granddaughter, whom he loved, was eight years old when he died, yet she had had no teaching, he left no provision for her education although he was rich, and in her mature womanhood she couldn't write and couldn't tell her husband's manuscript from anybody else's—she thought it was Shakespeare's.

When Shakespeare died in Stratford *it was not an event*. It made no more stir in England than the death of any other forgotten theatre-actor would have made. Nobody came down from London; there were no lamenting poems, no eulogies, no national tears—there was merely silence, and nothing more. A striking contrast with what happened when Ben Jonson, and Francis Bacon, and Spenser, and Raleigh and the other distinguished literary folk of Shakespeare's time passed from life! No praiseful voice was lifted for the lost Bard of Avon; even Ben Jonson waited seven years before he lifted his.

So far as anybody actually knows and can prove, Shakespeare of Stratford-on-Avon never wrote a play in his life.

So far as anybody knows and can prove, he never wrote a letter to anybody in his life.

So far as any one knows, he received only one letter during his life.

So far as any one *knows and can prove*, Shakespeare of Stratford wrote only one poem during his life. This one is authentic. He did write that one—a fact which stands undisputed; he wrote the whole of it; he wrote the whole of it out of his own head. He commanded that this work of art be engraved upon his tomb, and he was obeyed. There it abides to this day. This is it:

Good friend for Iesus sake forbeare
To digg the dust encloased heare:
Blest be ye man yt spares thes stones
And curst be he yt moves my bones.

In, the list as above set down, will be found *every positively known* fact of Shakespeare's life, lean and meagre as the invoice is. Beyond these details we know *not a thing* about him. All the rest of his vast history, as furnished by the biographers, is built up, course upon course, of guesses, inferences, theories, conjectures—an Eiffel Tower of artificialities rising sky-high from a very flat and very thin foundation of inconsequential facts. . . .

When Shakespeare died, in 1616, great literary productions attributed to him as author had been before the London world and in high favor for twenty-four years. Yet his death was not an event. It made no stir, it attracted no attention. Apparently his eminent literary contemporaries did not realize that a celebrated poet had passed from their midst. Perhaps they knew a play-actor of minor rank had disappeared, but did not regard him as the author of his Works. "We are justified in assuming" this.

His death was not even an event in the little town of Stratford. Does this mean that in Stratford he was not regarded as a celebrity of *any* kind?

"We are privileged to assume"—no, we are indeed *obliged* to assume—that such was the case. He had spent the first twenty-two or twenty-three years of his life there, and of course knew everybody and was known by everybody of that day in the town, including the dogs and the cats and the horses. He had spent the last five or six years of his life there, diligently trading in every big and little thing that had money in it; so we are compelled to assume that many of the folk there in those said latter days knew him personally, and the rest by sight and hearsay. But not as a *celebrity?* Apparently not. For everybody soon forgot to remember any contact with him or any incident connected with him. The dozens of townspeople, still alive, who had known of him or known about him in the first twenty-three years of his life were in the same unremembering condition: if they knew of any incident connected with that period of his life they didn't tell about it. Would they if they had been asked? It is most likely. Were they asked? It is pretty apparent that they were not. Why weren't they? It is a very plausible guess that nobody there or elsewhere was interested to know.

For seven years after Shakespeare's death nobody seems to have been interested in him. Then the quarto[15] was published, and Ben Jonson awoke out of his long indifference and sang a song of praise and put it in the front of the book. Then silence fell *again*.

For sixty years. Then inquiries into Shakespeare's Stratford life began to be made, of Stratfordians. Of Stratfordians who had known Shakespeare or had seen him? No. Then of Stratfordians who had seen people who had known or seen people who had seen Shakespeare? No. Apparently the inquiries were only made of Stratfordians who were not Stratfordians of Shakespeare's day, but later comers; and what they had learned had come to them from persons who had not seen Shakespeare; and what they had learned was not claimed as *fact*, but only as legend—dim and fading and indefinite legend; legend of the calf-slaughtering rank, and not worth remembering either as history or fiction.

Has it ever happened before—or since—that a celebrated person who had spent exactly half of a fairly long life in the village where he was born

---

15. **quarto** book with pages nine by twelve inches

and reared, was able to slip out of this world and leave that village voiceless and gossipless behind him—utterly voiceless, utterly gossipless? And permanently so? I don't believe it has happened in any case except Shakespeare's. And couldn't and wouldn't have happened in his case if he had been regarded as a celebrity at the time of his death.

When I examine my own case—but let us do that, and see if it will not be recognizable as exhibiting a condition of things quite likely to result, most likely to result, indeed substantially *sure* to result in the case of a celebrated person, a benefactor of the human race. Like me.

My parents brought me to the village of Hannibal, Missouri, on the banks of the Mississippi, when I was two and a half years old. I entered school at five years of age, and drifted from one school to another in the village during nine and a half years. Then my father died, leaving his family in exceedingly straitened circumstances; wherefore my book-education came to a standstill forever, and I became a printer's apprentice, on board and clothes, and when the clothes failed I got a hymn-book in place of them. This for summer wear, probably. I lived in Hannibal fifteen and a half years, altogether, then ran away, according to the custom of persons who are intending to become celebrated. I never lived there afterward. Four years later I became a "cub" on a Mississippi steamboat in the St. Louis and New Orleans trade, and after a year and a half of hard study and hard work the U.S. inspectors rigorously examined me through a couple of long sittings and decided that I knew every inch of the Mississippi—thirteen hundred miles—in the dark and in the day—as well as a baby knows the way to its mother's paps day or night. So they licensed me as a pilot—knighted me, so to speak—and I rose up clothed with authority, a responsible servant of the United States government.

Now then. Shakespeare died young—he was only fifty-two. He had lived in his native village twenty-six years, or about that. He died celebrated (if you believe everything you read in the books). Yet when he died nobody there or elsewhere took any notice of it, and for sixty years afterward no townsman remembered to say anything about him or about his life in Stratford. When the inquirer came at last he got but one fact—no, *legend*—and got that one at second hand, from a person who had only heard it as a rumor, and didn't claim copyright in it as a production of his own. He couldn't, very well, for its date antedated[16] his own birth-date. But necessarily a number of persons were still alive in Stratford who, in the days of their youth, had seen Shakespeare nearly every day in the last five years of his life, and they would have been able to tell that inquirer some first-hand things about him if he had in those days been a celebrity and therefore a

---

16. **antedated** preceded

person of interest to the villagers. Why did not the inquirer hunt them up and interview them? Wasn't it worth while? Wasn't the matter of sufficient consequence? Had the inquirer an engagement to see a dog-fight and couldn't spare the time?

It all seems to mean that he never had any literary celebrity, there or elsewhere, and no considerable repute as actor and manager.

Now then, I am away along in life—my seventy-third year being already well behind me—yet *sixteen* of my Hannibal schoolmates are still alive today, and can tell—and do tell—inquirers dozens and dozens of incidents of their young lives and mine together; things that happened to us in the morning of life, in the blossom of our youth, in the good days, the dear days, "the days when we went gipsying, a long time ago." Most of them creditable to me, too. One child to whom I paid court when she was five years old and I eight still lives in Hannibal, and she visited me last summer, traversing the necessary ten or twelve hundred miles of railroad without damage to her patience or to her old-young vigor. Another little lassie to whom I paid attention in Hannibal when she was nine years old and I the same, is still alive—in London—and hale and hearty, just as I am. And on the few surviving steamboats—those lingering ghosts and remembrancers of great fleets that plied the big river in the beginning of my water-career—which is exactly as long ago as the whole invoice of the life-years of Shakespeare number—there are still findable two or three river-pilots who saw me do creditable things in those ancient days; and several white-headed engineers; and several roustabouts and mates; and several deckhands who used to heave the lead for me and send up on the still night air the "six—feet—*scant!*" that made me shudder, and the "M-a-r-k—*twain!*" that took the shudder away, and presently the darling "By the d-e-e-p—*four!*"[17] that lifted me to heaven for joy. They know about me, and can tell. And so do printers, from St. Louis to New York; and so do newspaper reporters, from Nevada to San Francisco. And so do the police. If Shakespeare had really been celebrated, like me, Stratford could have told things about him; and if my experience goes for anything, they'd have done it.

---

17. **four** four fathoms, or twenty-four feet

Tim Clark

"Those Huddled Masses"

In this magazine article, Tim Clark describes a harrowing nineteenth-century shipwreck and the tense rescue at sea that followed.

FOR five days, the cargo steamer *Missouri* had battled stiff westerly winds and high seas on its voyage from London to Philadelphia. Captain Hamilton Murrell of the Atlantic Transport Line was disgusted to learn that in the twenty-four hours preceding his noon sighting of April 5, 1889, the *Missouri* had covered only 134 miles—half a normal day's run. Murrell, though only twenty-three years old, was a veteran of twelve years in the merchant service, and the *Missouri* was his second command. But unless conditions improved, this was not going to be a profitable voyage.

An hour later Murrell's brooding[1] was interrupted by his Third Officer, Mr. Lucas. Lucas had spotted a large steamer one point off the port bow, apparently in distress. Murrell altered his course to approach the stricken vessel.

It was the *Danmark* of Copenhagen, en route to New York with 665 passengers, most of them Norwegian emigrants with families, and a crew of some seventy men. The day before, a propeller shaft had broken loose, killing her chief engineer and tearing a huge hole in the ship's bottom before her engines could be stopped. As onrushing seawater threatened to overwhelm what pumps were still in operation, the *Danmark's* skipper, Captain Knudsen, asked Murrell if he could take off the passengers.

Murrell was flabbergasted. He had a crew of thirty-seven plus a few passengers, and might have been able to squeeze in another twenty or so, but the thought of taking on almost 700 was absurd. He offered instead to tow

1. **brooding** worrying anxiously

the *Danmark* to the nearest port, which was St. John's in Newfoundland. Knudsen accepted, and the crews of the two ships got busy with the complicated operation. Taking a ship in tow in mid-ocean is not like taking a car in tow on land. Imagine trying to attach a tow line to the other car's bumper during an earthquake when both vehicles are rolling back and forth, and rocking from side to side. Now imagine those vehicles thousands of times larger and heavier, and one begins to appreciate the difficulties involved.

Murrell steered the *Missouri* to windward of the crippled liner, and a boat from the *Danmark* brought over one end of a three-inch-thick manila rope. Once aboard the *Missouri*, it was used to haul over a monstrous ten-inch cable, which once transferred was secured to mooring posts, or "bitts" on the forecastle[2] deck. The tow rope was 120 fathoms[3] (720 feet) long, and on board the *Danmark* it was attached to another forty fathoms of anchor chain, so that the two ships, underway with the tow line taut, were about a thousand feet apart.

The operation was concluded by 4:30 that afternoon. Now the *Missouri*, steaming at its slowest speed so as to take up the enormous strain without any sudden jerks that could part the cable, turned the *Danmark* into the wind, and began heading into the waves on a course west-northwest, with St. John's some 650 miles away.

As night fell, lanterns were hung over the *Missouri's* stern[4] to aid the steersmen[5] aboard the *Danmark*. In the continued heavy seas, the strain on the tow line was frightful. A wire bridle[6] was added to the line where it was tied to the *Missouri's* mooring bitts, but a gigantic wave smashed into the bow at about 11:30 that night, and carried the bridle away. The beams of the forecastle deck itself were pried up by the blow, and for a moment the *Missouri* shuddered and groaned like an animal in pain. But the tow line held, and in a few hours the wind had moderated enough to allow another wire bridle put on the cable. By dawn, wind and waves had diminished so much that the *Missouri* could increase its speed.

But the first light of April 6 revealed a new and deadly obstacle—ice. Captain Murrell realized that there was no way his laboring ship could force its way through the pack ice to be expected at that time of year in those latitudes. Reluctantly he ordered a change of course. The two ships reversed themselves and headed for the Azores, more than a thousand miles south and east.

---

2. **forecastle** part of a ship's upper deck forward of the foremast
3. **fathom** measurement equal to six feet
4. **stern** rear part of a ship
5. **steersmen** navigators
6. **bridle** metal restraint

As he gave the order, Captain Murrell must have wondered if his ship could endure the strain of dragging the much larger *Danmark* all the way to the Azores. But he needn't have worried. The *Danmark* was not going any farther. At 8:30 that morning, Captain Knudsen signaled: "AM LEAKING BADLY—FIVE FEET OF WATER IN AFTERHOLD." Half an hour later came a second message: "AM SINKING—TAKE OFF MY PEOPLE."

There was no longer any choice about it, and only one way it could be done. Captain Murrell ordered his men to throw the entire cargo—cement, linseed, bundles of rags, bales of wool, indigo,[7] herring,[8] and skins—overboard. The tow line was cut, and the desperate people on board the *Danmark* were ordered to stand by to be taken off—women and children first. No baggage allowed. Murrell ordered two officers, Lucas and Forsyth, to take the *Missouri's* two lifeboats over to the *Danmark* and assist with the evacuation. He also ordered them to make sure that every boatload brought as much food as possible from the sinking ship. The *Missouri* had a freshwater condenser[9] capable of producing 8,000 gallons of drinking water a day, but there were provisions only for forty men for three weeks. Now began the most dangerous phase of the rescue. In all there were 735 persons on board the doomed *Danmark*—twenty-two of them babies less than a year old, sixty-five children under twelve, and 200 women. There were eight lifeboats, each capable of carrying twenty-three or twenty-four persons, and a smaller boat that was used exclusively for provisions.

A quarter-mile of ocean separated the two ships, and a heavy swell from the southwest made transferring passengers from ship to boat and back to ship tricky. Mr. Forsyth was knocked down into his boat while trying to fend off from the side of the *Danmark*, and lost seven teeth. Had he fallen between the boat and the ship, he would have been crushed.

The *Danmark* had an accommodation ladder that could be used by older passengers, and the sailors on board the *Missouri* had rigged ropes and nets on her side, but getting the babies and small children from ship to boat and back again presented a problem. Captain Murrell came up with an ingenious[10] solution. The children were placed in coal baskets and hauled up and down with ropes. By 10:15 A.M., the first boatload had arrived at the *Missouri*—two women and twenty-two infants, plus one large doll which a young owner had refused to leave behind. They were swung up on deck, where the sailors, unsure of how to handle them, put them all in the saloon cabin on the deck. When the other mothers arrived on the next boat, they

---

7. **indigo** plants that produce dark blue dye
8. **herring** type of fish
9. **condenser** apparatus that changes a gas or vapor into liquid
10. **ingenious** clever

found their babies rolling helplessly to and fro on the reeling floor of the cabin, squalling but safe.

By noon, all the women and children had been transferred, and the men began to come across. Murrell had the challenging task of continually keeping far enough away from the *Danmark* to avoid a collision. At times, the waves were so high that the boats disappeared from view in the deep valleys between crests.

The last boatload of passengers came aboard the *Missouri* at 4:30 that afternoon. The weather was worsening, and a light rain was turning to fog as Captain Knudsen, who had stayed on board the *Danmark* to direct the transfer operation, abandoned his ship. His last act was to shoot three valuable dogs that were being shipped to America. There was no telling whether there would be enough food for the people, so the dogs had to be sacrificed. At 5:30, the fog enveloped the *Danmark*, and the *Missouri* got underway. There being no room for them on board, the *Danmark's* six boats were scuttled,[11] so that no other ship, coming across them in mid-ocean, would report the steamer lost with all hands. As it turned out, one of the *Missouri's* sister ships, the *Minnesota*, did spot some of the wreckage, and took the grim tidings to London.

Now it fell to the *Missouri's* chief officer, Mr. Gates, to find accommodations for the crowd. The officers and men of the *Missouri* gave up their berths[12] to the frailest of the women and children. Captain Murrell's cabin was taken over by five women and a baby, while eleven young girls were squeezed into the 6'x12' wheelhouse. The empty cargo hold was crammed with refugees, and about two hundred were left to sleep on the deck, protected from the elements by sails, awnings,[13] and tarpaulins.[14] By midnight all were bedded down, in varying degrees of comfort, and the ship was running before a fresh gale towards her destination.

But the long day's labor and excitement were not over yet. At 1 A.M., a passenger gave birth to a baby girl in the chief officer's berth, assisted by the ship's doctor. (She was named Atlanta Missourie Linnie.)

It was a difficult night. The wind increased to a strong gale, and heavy seas washed over the unfortunate people on the deck. There was no hope of changing wet clothes, and no dry clothes to put on. Now that the exhilarating rescue was over, many of the emigrants had time to realize the enormity of their losses—all their possessions, and in many cases their life savings.

---

11. **scuttled** sent to bottom; sunk
12. **berths** sleeping accomodations
13. **awnings** coverings
14. **tarpaulins** waterproofed canvases

It was a cold and comfortless dawn as the passengers, jammed on the main deck, walked up and down disconsolately,[15] trying to warm themselves and work out kinks in stiff muscles. Everyone was soaked to the bone, and mothers could only try to comfort their crying babies with murmurs and embraces.

But there was food enough for everyone—butter, cheese, biscuits, German sausage, and hot coffee. The people lined up for their provisions and shuffled through the galley for coffee, which was ladled out into buckets, meat tins, saucepan lids, and in some cases directly into open mouths. A tub of rice was boiled for the children, who sat around it with their mothers. Later that morning, Captain Murrell turned the ship into the freshening breeze so that clothing and sails could be dried, and for a while the *Missouri* looked like a floating clothesline.

As the day went on the weather improved, and with food and dried clothing, so did the spirits of those on board. It was a Sunday, and that evening several Lutheran preachers who were among the emigrants held a service of thanksgiving. One of the *Danmark's* cabin passengers, a Miss Lofgrin of the "Swedish Quartette," was a professional singer, and she sang for the gathering among other songs, "Home Sweet Home."

The next day was also fine, and the seas were calm enough to allow the crew to improvise washtubs by cutting hogsheads[16] in half. The passengers had a chance to wash themselves, everyone had three meals, and there was more worship and singing on the deck that night. The *Missouri* was making good time, and at 10 the next morning, April 9, land was sighted. It was Terceira, one of the Azores. Captain Murrell laid a course for Ponta Delgado, a harbor on the island of St. Michael's, and there was one more night of prayers, songs, and hardship before the anchor was let down on the morning of April 10.

Once on land, Captain Murrell met with the Danish consul, who told him that the mail steamer, the only form of communication with the mainland, had left the day before, and it would be two weeks before it would return. The consul and Captain Knudsen asked Murrell if he would allow some of the passengers to continue on to America on the *Missouri*. Murrell agreed, and it was decided that 365—about half, all women, children, and married men—could stay on board, and head directly for Philadelphia, while the rest, all single men, were put ashore and quartered in an empty grain warehouse, where they would stay until the owners of the *Danmark* could provide alternate transport to New York.

---

15. **disconsolately** very sadly

16. **hogheads** large barrels

Meanwhile, the *Missouri* was taking on fresh provisions, including two bullocks,[17] a dozen sheep, a ton of fresh meat, twelve dozen chickens, a thousand eggs, biscuits, bread, fruit, vegetables, flour, rice, more blankets, and eating utensils. Captain Murrell promised his crew an extra month's pay in return for putting up with more crowding for the ten-day run. By sunset of the next day, April 11, the *Missouri* was underway again, leaving the harbor to the cheers of the islanders and the Norwegians on land and aboard ship.

The voyage to America was unremarkable. The crew made Easter eggs for the children on Good Friday, and the wrecks of two other ships were sighted on April 20. On Sunday, April 21, a last religious service was held, and at nine o'clock that night the pilot boat *Henry Cope* met the *Missouri* off Cape Henlopen. The long journey was over.

By now news of the rescue had been telegraphed and cabled around the world, and a huge crowd lined the banks of the Delaware River the next day as the *Missouri* made its way upriver to Philadelphia. Hundreds of steam whistles screeched in welcome, reporters flocked aboard the ship from small boats to get exclusives, and a crowd of five thousand strong waited on the wharf, cheering.

The passengers were eventually reunited with those who had been left in the Azores, who arrived in New York a month later. The Atlantic Transport Line approved Captain Murrell's actions, and gave the crew their bonus, as he had promised them. Murrell became the toast of the East Coast, and honors and decorations flooded in from around the world. The kings of Sweden and Rumania sent gold medals, Prince Bismarck of Germany sent a congratulatory letter, and the king of Denmark made Murrell a Knight of the Order of Dannebrog.

Murrell's rewards were not limited to the praise of princes. In the crowd that came to welcome the hero to Baltimore a few weeks later was a young woman who, shortly after meeting him, became his wife, and eventually bore him six children. The Murrells moved in 1901 to Massachusetts, where he worked for the Baltimore-Boston Barge Company.

Hamilton Murrell died of rheumatic fever in 1916, just four years after another passenger liner signaled desperately for rescue in the North Atlantic. But this time help came too late, and more than fifteen hundred passengers of the *Titanic* drowned, twenty-three years to the month after the rescue of the *Danmark*.

Author's Note: This article was adapted from material originally written

---

17. **bullocks** bulls; steers

by Catherine Murrell, the captain's mother, and privately printed in 1891. Catherine Murrell's account was supplied to *Yankee* courtesy of Esther Brittain Fry (Mrs. William J. Fry). She received it from Captain Murrell's son, Eric Hamilton Murrell, who is her uncle by marriage.